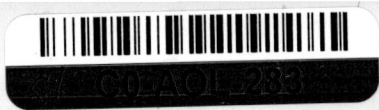

CONCILIUM

THEOLOGY IN THE AGE OF RENEWAL

CONCILIUM

CONCILIUM/VOL. 9

SPIRITUALITY

SPIRITUALITY
IN
CHURCH
AND
WORLD

Volume 9

CONCILIUM
theology in the age of renewal

PAULIST PRESS
NEW YORK, N.Y. / GLEN ROCK, N.J.

NIHIL OBSTAT: Joseph F. Donahue, S.J., S.T.D.
Censor Deputatus

IMPRIMATUR: ✠ Bernard J. Flanagan, D.D.
Bishop of Worcester

October 21, 1965

The Nihil Obstat and Imprimatur are official declarations that a book or pamphlet is free of doctrinal or moral error. No implication is contained therein that those who have granted the Nihil Obstat and Imprimatur agree with the contents, opinions or statements expressed.

Library of Congress Catalogue Card Number: 65-28868

Suggested Decimal Classification: 291.4

BOOK DESIGN: Claude Ponsot

Paulist Press assumes responsibility for the accuracy of the English translations in this Volume.

PAULIST PRESS
EXECUTIVE OFFICES: 304 W. 58th Street, New York, N.Y. and
    21 Harristown Road, Glen Rock, N.J.
Executive Publisher: John A. Carr, C.S.P.
Executive Manager: Alvin A. Illig, C.S.P.
Asst. Executive Manager: Thomas E. Comber, C.S.P.

EDITORIAL OFFICES: 304 W. 58th Street, New York, N.Y.
Editor: Kevin A. Lynch, C.S.P.
Managing Editor: Urban P. Intondi

Printed and bound in the United States of America by The Colonial Press Inc., Clinton, Mass.

CONTENTS

PREFACE

Christian Duquoc, O.P./*Lyons, France*

The present volume is devoted to "spirituality". The term is vague. We might say that it refers to Christian life insofar as we wish to discover in this life certain directives by which to guide ourselves in practice. Occasionally "spirituality" is contrasted with theology or with Christian thought in the broad sense. Often accused of being unrealistic or ineffectual, it has not much of a reputation among men of action or "pastors".

Is it merely a matter of option, something destined for a few initiates who have been granted a special charisma? Is it but a certain cast of mind which some are fortunate or unfortunate enough to have, and others not? Does it necessarily imply a break with the world, a break it is said to delight in? Is it so unamenable to all reflection that the only thing a theologian can do is to wash his hands of it? Is it so uninterested in its age, so indifferent to human history, that the apostle or the man of action does not know what to do with it? Is it merely the business of monks? And must the layman who labors enthusiastically at the humanization of the world abandon all hope of ever becoming a "spiritual" man? Must he be content with being a second-rate Christian, or must he become an "exile" with no interest in his surroundings?

This volume does not pretend to answer all these questions.

1

One cannot release tensions created by the social, political, cultural and religious factors of a given age merely by writing articles. At Vatican Council II the Church has taken cognizance of a new form of existence in the world. Not that the Church makes the Gospel suit the fashion. She wants to take up a different position in the world in order to make her witness to the Gospel more effective. This volume recognizes that new situation. It takes note of the difficulties created by this new situation in connection with "spirituality" as ordinary Christians usually understand it. These difficulties are collective rather than individual. That is why the various contributions concentrate more on the way our Christian existence is conditioned by ideologies and collective behavior than on the factors in "individual fallen nature" which prevent it from opening up in the grace of Christ, since these factors are sometimes looked upon as irrelevant to this age.

These collective difficulties are created by various factors: the emergence of the laity in the Church, the serious consideration given to non-Christian forms of spirituality, the failure of Christianity in the old, non-Western civilizations, the great number of spiritualities and the oneness of the Gospel.

These factors are examined here. The emergence of the laity in the Church is not merely an ecclesial phenomenon; it has arisen out of a general evolution in our civilization. It means the emergence of a new type of spirituality, not different from the others insofar as it is rooted in the Gospel, but distinct from them in that it embraces the whole human reality. The laity have not yet fully realized their place in the Church; they have not yet created their own type of spiritual existence. Their situation is still unstable.

This instability has its repercussions on the priesthood and religious life. Until the emergence of the laity, the spirituality of the clergy envisioned itself in control, and the religious found their niche in the evangelical counsels. But from now on every believer claims the same fidelity to the Christian message. What seemed settled once for all now seems to dissolve.

The difficulties created by the recognition of non-Christian forms of spirituality are no less: it may tend to an underrating of the originality of Christian life. And the failure of Christianity in the old civilizations seems to provide concrete proof that these forms of spirituality are so firmly embedded in the deepest layers of human society and that Christianity is so peculiar or special that it is incapable of integrating them.

Lastly, the very multiplicity of "spiritualities" within Christendom pushes the evangelical foundation of Christian life into the background. Hans Urs von Balthasar shows, with no lack of vigor, that the Gospel is the basis of all spirituality. In this time of change it is ultimately the Gospel that must decide how our Christian life will have to react in view of new cultural, social and political factors.

PART I

ARTICLES

Hans Urs von Balthasar/*Basle, Switzerland*

The Gospel as Norm and Test of All Spirituality in the Church

I

The Philosophical and Religious Precedents of the Notion of Spirituality

The notion of spirituality is a modern one, found neither in the tradition of religious philosophy nor of biblical theology. It is therefore important to determine its content and bearing. In general (negatively speaking) it may be said that there is no reason for the Christian to limit spirituality to the context of Christianity; just as Christians speak of a "medieval" or a "Carmelite" or a "lay" spirituality, so can we speak analogously of a "Buddhist" or a "Sufi" spirituality. On the basis of the same common understanding of the idea, spirituality may be approximately defined as that basic practical or existential attitude of man which is the consequence and expression of the way in which he understands his religious—or more generally, his ethically committed—existence; the way in which he acts and reacts habitually throughout his life according to his objective and ultimate insights and decisions. From this first delimitation of the notion it is not difficult to see that, even within the Christian context, it is not fully covered by "practical theology" which, in an objective and didactic manner, draws the practical conclusions for life from theoretic ("dogmatic") theology prior to any decisions taken by the individual; nor can it be identified

7

with "ascetic-mystical" theology which, according to its label if not always in fact, limits the personal application of fundamental religious decisions to specific "exercises" and "experiences".

Before we can, in a meaningful way, deal with the question whether there is only one Christian spirituality or more, we have to examine the precedents of this idea in the context of humanity at large, since the question of one or more "spiritualities" is equally relevant there. Here the word "spirituality" can at least give us some initial guidance: it is centered on the spirit, and its bearing embraces the usage of this term in antiquity (*nous,* from Anaxagoras to Plotinus), Christian usage (*pneuma-spiritus,* from the Alexandrines to the school of St. Victor, the "Spirituals", the Reformers and the Pietists), and modern usage (particularly in Hegel, as the subjective-objective implication of the notion of being).

This wide application is not necessarily formless and vague since the word always implies at least one basic and clear precision, namely, that man sees and defines himself in the light of his spiritual quality, and not of his material, bodily or instinctive aspects. The spirit opens up in an unequivocal yet mysterious way the totality of being, an absolute totality since the notion of relative being can only be the result of a relative view, from one particular point; or in other words, since the spirit's claim to truth necessarily implies the absolute. Here we have, therefore, the dimensions of human spirituality in principle.

(a) Man, who defines himself by his spiritual aspect (as distinct from world or animal), relates everything else he may be (a part of the world, a material organism) to his spirit. However problematic the tension between spirit and organism within him may appear, he cannot seriously consider himself as a dichotomy, consisting of two equally powerful halves with equal claims which he must seek to reduce to final harmony and unity. He is a single being, the center of which lies in his spirit which is in charge of the final harmony within himself and within the extent of his life. But what is this spirit in me, in all its purity and absoluteness? The first approach to an answer starts from what is dispersed to what is gathered together, from fallenness to "uprightness", from self-estrangement to the familiar—where we belong. It is the breakthrough of all thought toward the "theoria", insofar as this is the "philo-sophical", existential search for the truth of existence. It is the way of India, Plato, Plotinus, Augustine, Descartes and Fichte. Insofar as it implies the basic search for an absolute point of reference, above all in one's own spirit and in the depth of one's will, and the need to relate everything to this absolute point of reference, spirituality is, first of all: *eros,* or "the inward way", or *anamnesis* and *elpis,* or, insofar as everything that is not this absolute center of the spirit is ruthlessly reduced to a merely relative position: a teaching about death.

(b) But merely relating all things to the spirit in me is not enough. The spirit wants to express itself in reality. Formally speaking, it wants to become the total content within everything relative. Only in this way does the "relation to the absolute" become principally a "decision". In his *Meno* Plato developed the formal point of reference, in his *Symposium* he showed how *eros* strives toward it, but it is in his *Republic* that he worked out the application of the spirit to the whole of reality, whether individual or social, and this he does by means of the "cardinal virtues" as the principles on which this spiritual order is based.

It is here that the dominance of the spirit is shown not to be a matter of arbitrariness and exploitation (as the sophists and ruling class maintained in the first books of the *Republic*) but rather of factual objectivity and selfless service to reality. Only thus can the natural and bodily environment be given moral significance (*ethizesthai:* Aristotle). In this widening service of the world and in such consistent "objectivization" the subjective spirit can attain its own absolute value (Hegel). In this constant listening to the widening law of being the spirit can "hear" itself (Heidegger). By letting the absolute exist in itself as an inexhaustible "idea" the spirit molds reality (Kant). This stage does not deny the "teaching about death" contained in "eros", but introduces it into the world, where this "dying" becomes indeed a matter to be taken seriously. Without the world as a "matter for duty" (Fichte) the spirit would remain a dream and would never become itself in "action".

(c) But all this can only be accomplished when the acting person does not take his nostalgia for the absolute (eros) as his norm, because this nostalgia as such is still subjective. He must allow the absolute to be in command as the norm-giving spirit, and this not merely as a formal maxim within my own spirit (Aristotle, Kant), but as the concrete absolute Mind (Logos), which my limited mind still sees as formal and abstract, and only becomes concrete when my mind allows the absolute Truth to choose, to be, to "happen" within myself. This is, after the "eros spirituality" of Plato and those influenced by him and the "appropriate action spirituality" of Aristotle and his school, the spirituality of the Stoa (and all those schools with a similar attitude: from the *apatheia* of Zen and India and the Fathers of the Church to the resignation of the German mystics, the "indifference" of Ignatius and the "pure love" of Fénélon). No wonder that Epictetus meant for Pascal the final achievement of ancient existential thought. Existence under the lasting judgment of the Logos (as Marcus Aurelius tried to live it somehow) is not a mere transplantation to Plato's place of the divine ideas, nor Aristotle's self-alienation in an objective working world; it is broken from one moment to another, and constantly judged as at the moment of death by the inexorable judgment of the absolute Logos which confronts the supreme effort of man as the free action of the absolute Mind in my mind. This should not be read as an anticipation of the Christian attitude by the pagan one, which is historically unjustifiable, but as the objective implication of what is necessarily involved in the fundamental recognition of an absolute spiritual principle in any serious human spirituality.

II

THE MARKS OF A UNIVERSALLY HUMAN SPIRITUALITY

The intertwining of these three forms of human spirituality must be seen as a unity. Every new aspect arises from the preceding one and can, in turn, again be integrated in the preceding one, however much one or other particular accent tries to become absolute according to the various tendencies or schools. It is therefore superficial and "scholastic" to dispose of those philosophies that are concerned with the reconciliation of these various tendencies (glibly described as Platonism, Aristotelianism and Stoicism) by contemptuously labelling them as "syncretistic". The concrete or syncretic element is rather the common ground of all philosophy and spirituality, and it is this common ground which I wish to investigate a little further.

(a) From the point of view of Plato's *eros,* Augustine's *desiderium,* or Thomas's *amor-appetitus,* the spirit appears as essentially transcendental, insofar as it partakes of absoluteness by *moving away* from itself toward the absolute. Next, this transcendence is reflected in its relation to the objective world outside, in unselfish *service;* and thirdly, it is contained in *allowing* the absolute Mind to *exist freely* within me. Insofar as this transcending (*philo-sophia*) toward the real "Being" (*logos*) is the spiritual soul (*psychē*), there is no room apart from this philosophy for an equivalent claim of a closed system of psychology that also contains, recaptures and reflects such a movement of the spirit away from itself (as is somewhat the case with C. G. Jung, and others). From a deeper point of view, even the Indian-Platonic movement on one's own level can have no effect because this "inward way" leads to no "arrival": this would limit the transcending and cancel the *eros* and *desiderium.*

In its later phase, therefore, Platonism characterized the spirit (*nous*) as the longing of being for the absolute (*Hen*—the One). Such was the view of Plotinus and Gregory of Nyssa. Any reflection, which would attempt to contain this movement within "psychology" as its norm, would suppress the movement and itself with it (this was Bergson's problem). But the same is done by any "mysticism" which would seek a norm for the *eros* movement in a psychical experience. Such a norm would close the way for the second form of spirituality, the self-realization of the spirit through activity in this world, and make it impossible as can be seen in many systems of mysticism inside or outside the Christian context.

(b) Insofar as the "action" spirituality of Aristotle is concerned, it is utterly indispensable for the absolute *eros:* it is in the world that the *eros* finds the *locus* for its exercise, conservation, education and purification. For man this *locus* or "field of operation" is necessarily twofold: it contains the *eros* of "I" and "Thou", and this both on the sexual and the supra-sexual (friendship) level, and it is the *eros* as the gift of oneself to the community (people, State, mankind) and to the common activity of this mankind (culture, technical development, progress). This dual aspect lies in man's being: in the body he is an individual person, and at the same time as spirit he tends toward the universal as an obligation. One can emphasize the first relationship (Feuerbach, Buber), or the second (Marx), or both (Fichte), but in every case man is orientated, by the very structure of the *eros,* toward his fellowman and work in the world, because his *eros* demands the concrete fulfillment of his spirit, although the *eros* cannot completely lose itself in this relationship with fellowman and world. And so we find in the middle of the *Republic* the parable of the cave and the sun of goodness.

(c) It is in the spirituality of allowing the absolute freedom of action (*Geschehenlassen*) that we finally are confronted with the whole abyss of the problem of human spirituality: what is the relationship between the human spirit and the absolute Spirit? Platonism contains a kind of naive theism, which carries and includes the transcending movement of the spirit as its origin and its goal; Aristotelianism implies a kind of naive a-theism insofar as the ethical inclination toward the world (in the

"I" and "Thou" relationship and in culture) provisionally post-
pones the problem of God to a later stage. But Stoicism poses
the unavoidable question whether man himself or God contains
this absolute mind. This leads to the question whether spirituality is ultimately a monologue (pantheism) or a dialogue and
a prayer. It is still a monologue when the tension between the
absolute mind and the individual mind is seen as a tension between man as a *noumenon* and man as a *phenomenon*. But
there is dialogue when the Stoa (*e.g.,* in Cleanthes' prayer) in-
terprets itself in the light of the old mythical religion. In this
last case Stoic spirituality becomes a kind of recapitulation of
all human spiritualities insofar as there is room in it also for the
tension of the Platonic *eros* and for the outward inclination
toward the world of Aristotle.

Even then the three basic forms remain relatively independent, *i.e.,* the one cannot be completely reduced to the other, and
so they show precisely that the human way of being is not
absolute, in other words, they show that the transcending movement is a constitutive element of it, whether this transcending
leads to God or to the world, so that human "perfection" can
never coincide with the absolute mind and truth except in that
openness, that readiness and that receptivity which leave to
God that complete primacy over man and world that is his by
right.

Man, subject to original sin, can absolutize anything, even
this moment of creaturely "indifference" which he can put on a
level with the way God surpasses every difference (*coincidentia
oppositorum*), and so puts what is least divine on a level with
what is most divine (Heraclitus, Giordano Bruno, Schelling).
But in itself the structure of man's limitations shows man's
relativeness plainly enough so as to put a claim to absoluteness
against a possible divine revelation out of the question. However genuine the intellectual preamble of a human spirituality
may be, its content cannot constitute a limitation or indispensable condition of the biblical revelation.

III

THE SPIRITUALITY OF THE BIBLE AND OF JESUS CHRIST

The question of the relationship between God and man, which is either ignored or wrongly put, is settled in the Bible from God's point of view. On the supreme level of his Word, God chooses, promises, demands, rejects and fulfills. And so, in the Old Testament, the three forms of natural spirituality are incorporated and used. *Eros* no longer finds its norm in itself, since its self-centered expectation of the divine does not correspond to the expectation of the true God, and in the "covenant" this norm now becomes a demand for loyalty. Man must no longer listen to his nostalgia for the divine in himself but in God's Word. Action is led beyond all purely human self-realization and becomes obedience to God and law, and this obedience contains a very concrete will of God which demands fulfillment in fellowship, among people, in the world. Lastly, resignation, guided by God's Word, becomes a faith ready to accept all and a patience ready to endure all, even the dark suffering of Israel as the Servant of God. Thus the one Word of God links all three forms of spirituality closer together within a full interrelationship. Here, however, we can still distinguish a difference of accent between "prophetic", "action and law" and "suffering and endurance".

Nevertheless, the initial guidance of God's Word in the Old Testament is but an introduction to Jesus Christ in the sense that the primacy and example of his humanity can and must be understood and received as the free and sovereign expression of God's Word. As Christ is man, the human forms of spirituality become again more evident in him than was the case in the Old Testament. But insofar as his Person is the revelation of a divine Person, these human forms of spirituality are constantly at the service of the revelation of the Trinitarian life within God himself. It is now the mission of every aspect of human nature in concrete history to serve to its full extent the expression of this divine Word.

If we start from the human nature of Christ insofar as it recapitulates (through Mary and the popular tradition) the human condition of the Old Testament, then Christ becomes, in his fulfillment of Plato's *eros-theoria* and the Old Testament fidelity to the covenant, the perfect way to the Father, thriving on this vision (*anamnesis* and *elpis*), clinging in love and prayer to every wish of the Father, relating everything to him and down from him.

In the same way, by fulfilling Aristotle's "practical" spirituality and his *arete* as well as the law of the Old Testament "to the last iota", Christ embodies that readiness in body and soul for God's work in the world. Hence, through this absolute commitment, God can achieve his salvation. Thirdly, by fulfilling the resignation of the Stoa and the utter surrender of the Servant of God in the Old Testament, Christ becomes he who is prepared to endure and suffer all things. And so God's own being and love and choice can become visible as through a transparent body.

It is true that all this is once for all realized in Jesus since he alone is the Son and the Revealer of the Father in the full sense; it is nevertheless obvious that for the expression of Christ's revelation this fulfillment of the human forms of spirituality is not a matter of indifference but rather an indispensable condition. These forms are, nevertheless, merely subordinate, even material, conditions, since the full form originates in the mission decreed by the Father. For it is not Jesus' love of the Father which, as such, constitutes the Word. Rather, Jesus and his love *is* the Word spoken by the Father, responded to in the Holy Spirit in a way that dominates the world's own response. Nor is Jesus' preparedness for the "absolute action" as such the work of salvation; it is rather God who has prepared this readiness so that God's readiness to redeem can be translated into effective action. Nor are Jesus' resignation to suffering and this suffering itself as such the grace of the Holy Spirit, although this grace cannot flow into the world except through the vessel of the previous and perfect readiness to receive God's saving will (which includes being abandoned on the cross and the descent into hell).

Insofar as Jesus' attitude is the once-for-all substratum of the self-revelation of the Trinity, it is and remains beyond any purely human imitation. But insofar as this same attitude has incorporated purely human basic attitudes, imitation—through grace—remains at the same time possible and is even required. And this is not merely an imitation from far off, at the vast distance between him who did all things for all men abundantly and those that hobble along and cannot add anything essential, if they add anything at all; but it is an imitation that incorporates the disciple in the original work through grace and in his predestined place.

This incorporation of human forms of spirituality in the expression of the revelation of the triune God of love implies a new foundation for these forms on the basis of an origin which is beyond their reach. The ("Platonic") *eros-desiderium,* which prefers God absolutely to anything in this world, becomes the expression of the triune love itself, insofar as the Son loves the Father in the Spirit in such a way that he puts him (the Father) and his love above everything. This new love expresses itself immediately in (Aristotle's) *praxis* and *arete* insofar as the Son sees in every human "Thou" the face of the Father (as the creator and lover of this human person) and so fulfills his task of universal redemption in the spirit of the same divine love. Lastly, this work, transcending its own capacity, is immediately carried through to the end, still always as the constantly overflowing love of the triune God for this world.

From this follows what is decisive for the Christian, namely, that the human (and now truly Christian) forms of spirituality can no longer be detached from the ultimate meaning which they have received in Christ's revelation. Henceforth, these various forms no longer have a kind of abstract and transcendent concept (which up till then could only be very imperfect and analogous), but the one, concrete norm is Jesus Christ who endows each of these forms with its own particular meaning derived from the unity of God's triune love.

I have already pointed out that these human forms of spirituality could not be reduced to each other, and that this showed up their relative and creaturely character. This remains true, but is overcome insofar as the unity of the divine revelation brings to this multiplicity of human attitudes such a supple unity in Jesus that it can become a supple unity for the manifestation of God's infinite love, somewhat like the unity of a musical scale or a color scale. And there can be no doubt that this supple unity of all human forms of spirituality in Christ must be called obedience in love (which becomes obedience in mission, work and suffering). In this christological center all possible forms of Christian spirituality meet and, through the medium of faith, flow into each other. They are but expressions of the one mission of Christ (which is his own absolute obedience in love) in the multiplicity of graces and tasks that he provides.

IV

THE LAW OF SHARING IN THIS SPIRITUALITY OF JESUS

When we now turn from the unity of all forms of spirituality in Jesus to their multiplicity in Church and mankind, then it follows from what has been said that it is a law that the spirituality of the Gospel cannot share with anything else in a kind of synthesis, as if it were but a part of a wider whole. There is therefore no question of bringing this Gospel spirituality into a synthesis with, for instance, a spirituality of "cultural progress" or of this "technical age", for which I, as "man of the twentieth century", would provide the unity and experience. From the Christian point of view the synthesis of God and world, and the concrete integration of the world on its way to God always lie in Christ.

Like all words of the Gospel, this is a "hard word". In order to understand it, it must be put back in the context of the Gospel. If this were but a religious philosophy for anybody or an abstract ethic for anybody, there would be no difficulty. But the inner meaning of the Gospel demands that man imitate Jesus in such a way that he stakes everything ultimately on this one card, abandoning the rest of the pack. He must leave everything, without looking back, without trying to create a synthesis between Jesus and leaving one's home, between Jesus and burying one's father, between Jesus and anything else. He must "take up his cross", that is, he must put the fulfillment of God's will before any other personal plans, preferences or attachments: father, mother, wife, child, home, field, etc. This refusal to synthesize, to compromise, is the rule, the measure, the "canon". Where this is understood and put into practice, where there is not merely "vocation" but "election" through positive response, there a life becomes "canonical", according to the "rule", in the Christian sense. In virtue of the indivisibility of his consent (or his existential faith) and of his existence such a man is "canonically" a Christian, a "saint", whether canonized by the Church or not. The saints set the standard for all the others; they are the judges of the world, already now but more still at the last judgment (1 Cor. 6, 1f.). They are the *analogatum princeps* (insofar as they embody the *forma Christi*) which provides the *perfecta ratio*[1] by which the other members of the comparison are measured. The existence of the saints takes away the guilt of the existence of others who compromise; this is the only way in which an (analogous) general concept of Christian existence is realized.

Since this *analogatum princeps* becomes the basic standard because of the Christian decision (to stake all on one card), this standard does not lie primarily in the neutrality of being sacramentally baptized, the darker side of which is very evident here, particularly insofar as the baptism of the unknowing child is concerned. This is significantly not mentioned in the New Testament. The least one can say in this connection is that a baptismal bond, not freely and fully accepted at the age of reason is for the Christian in question something wholly unclear and for others a wholly incredible and shocking riddle. Only in the case of such fringe phenomena of Christianity can people talk, apparently in good

[1] St. Thomas, *De Veritate* 1, 2c.

faith, of a "synthesis" of Christ and the world, of a Christian and a worldly existence.

The saints are those who imitate Christ in their lives according to the pattern of Christ's obedience in love, whatever status they have in the Church, or in whatever culture or technical age they exist. To try to discover another "canon" or rule or type of sanctity that would apparently be more up-to-date (*i.e.,* "synthetic"), is a complete illusion. This can also be seen in the fact that the effective "publicity" for occasional saints who live by this "canon" (and so could be canonized by the Church) is usually and directly undertaken by the Holy Spirit himself, while the purely ecclesiastical "publicity" (through canonization) comes frequently to nothing. There may well be changes in the outward form of this complete renouncement in order to enter into the perfection of Christ's obedience in love, but the fact itself cannot be affected, and is as much above time as the act of Christ belongs to all times till the end of the world.

V

The "Analogia Fidei"

It is Christ in glory who distributes offices, charismata and various tasks (Eph. 4, 9ff.), and he does this according to the "measure of the faith given" [2] beyond which one should not try to reach, and Christ himself is that all-embracing whole within which we are fitted as members "with gifts according to the grace given us . . . in proportion to our faith".[3] This proportion, measured by Christ himself (Rom. 12, 3ff.), is the only theological source of the many forms of spirituality.

As I have dealt elsewhere more extensively with this *analogia* (proportionality) within the Church,[4] a few indications may suf-

---

[2] *Hekastoi . . . emerisen metron pisteos.*
[3] *Kata tēn analogian tēs pisteos.*
[4] H. Urs von Balthasar, "Spiritualität," in *Skizzen zur Theologie I: Verbum Caro* (Einsiedeln, 1960-1).

fice here. Nothing in the Church is mere abstract principle: everything that is valid for all rests on concrete persons, or better, on concrete tasks entrusted to concrete persons ("pillars of the Church"). The Spirit of Christ shows the power of his oneness in the multiplicity of tongues (Acts 2), in the distribution of the various charismata (1 Cor. 12, 4), which show the riches of his inspiring oneness by their mutual relationship, as occasions for mutual service in love for the building up of the body of Christ (Eph. 4, 16).

The basic charisma is prior to all differentiation, and is that of the Church herself as the "Bride without blemish or wrinkle", chosen by Christ for himself, typified in Mary, the immaculate mother and bride insofar as she has a personal mission which as such is diffused by the Spirit and universalized into the principle of all that belongs to the Church (*Kirchlichkeit*).[5] Marian spirituality is then, properly understood, the same as the Church's spirituality, prior to all differentiation into individual charismata. As such it shows the true and general attitude that underlies all individual charismata, as the "spirituality of all spiritualities". Yet, with her "Behold the handmaid" this is nothing but the pure "feminine" response to the masculine "Thy will be done" of the new Adam: on her side pure transcendency, readiness for service and resignation, "canonically" fully corresponding to God. What this "formal" self-renouncement and response imply "materially" becomes clear in Luke's theologically stylized stories about Jesus' infancy, all mariological episodes: the spirit of bodily renouncement (virginity) in view of the Incarnation (Luke 1, 26-38), the spirit of the renouncement of material goods (poverty) in view of Christ's birth (Luke 2, 1-20), the spirit of renouncement of independence (obedience) to be subject to the law of the Lord (Luke 2, 21-40).

These are various expressions of renouncing, and so redeeming, love, which long before they came to mark out (as counsels) a particular status in the Church, already showed the uni-

---

[5] Cf. *idem*, "Wer ist die Kirche," in *Skizzen zur Theologie II: Sponsa Verbi* (Einsiedeln, 1960-1).

versal spirit of the Church and mariology in a love modelled on Christ. In the same way the spirituality of those who follow the counsels shows directly a spirituality of the universal Church in the hidden mystery of the bride; the spirituality of marriage (as a reflection of the original "type") is animated by the same spirit (Eph. 5, 21-33), a spirit in which the partners partake through the sacrament and which they must realize in their life; the spirituality of those in office must feed in the same Marian spirit on selfless service, and this almost without a new charismatic content being necessary, apart from the changed human condition.

In spite of this there are individual charismata, of which Paul enumerates several (Rom. 12, 6-8; 1 Cor. 12, 8-10), but he does so only to enclose them in the idea of service, and then, on a deeper level, in the idea of love. These gifts are sufficiently distinct to arouse possible jealousy among the members, but are otherwise sufficiently directed to the command of love to appear at once as fully valid expressions of this love. They are, therefore, not related to Christ as specific differences to a kind of distinct genus, but are, so to speak, new creative expressions of the concrete totality, not exclusive as rationally formulated individual functions within a natural or bodily community (as Paul's comparison with the body might suggest), but beyond that, as personal applications of Christ's grace given to individual persons. The charismata are not a system that can be "deduced", as is very clear from the original missions in the New Testament: Peter and John, Paul and James, but also Martha and Mary of Bethany, the evangelists, and the other less prominent apostles. All these charismata originated various applications of the Christian way of life which were all harmoniously linked with one another but which could not be reduced to mathematical deductions. The same holds for the great charismata that appear in Church history, as in the case of the founders of religious orders giving rise to quite definite spiritualities. And it holds again for doctors of the Church and other outstanding personalities who, like Augustine, Thomas, John of the Cross or Theresa of Lisieux, influenced Christianity beyond the limits of their day.

In all these cases it is important to look right through the newly opened window into the heart of the Gospel if we want to understand these phenomena in the sense meant by the Spirit. The more directly and profoundly this look leads to the Gospel, the more genuine is the spirituality, and the more it is in harmony with the Church. No one with a genuine mission has ever believed or intended that his message should proclaim a special and new spirituality. All attempts, therefore, of individuals or groups or categories to create their own spirituality and even to work it out in detail are suspect from the very start and in all probability sterile. Groups, which have not been endowed with prominent charismata, should be grateful to share in the anonymous service of the Church, Christ's handmaid.

To bring about alterations in the proportionate importance of missions in the Church is a matter for the Spirit of Christ: he alone knows how to shift the accent in any period in such a way that the rest does not suffer. When man tries to do this himself, he almost necessarily misjudges the situation and his work is most easily recognized by the resentment with which he tries to mark off his concern in connection with that of others. Those who want to heighten the value of marriage, rarely do so without throwing a shadow on evangelical virginity; those who are concerned with greater activity for the laity, only too easily attack the religious orders, particularly the contemplative ones. And yet, who can tell whether our times do not need precisely an intensification of contemplative life and a serious application to penance? And who does not see that a spirituality of a technological or progressive age is no spirituality at all as long as it is not fully covered and charged with the basic attitudes of the Gospel, as analyzed above?

And this leads us back to the question with which we started, the question of what may be called a spirituality of humanity as such, and the various basic forms arising from it. The ("Aristotelian") concentration on action leading to the recognition and conquest of nature was only one of three attitudes which belong inevitably to man's religious attitude. To make this concentration on action absolute means the impoverishment of man, particularly since this attitude contains a latent atheism. The human forms of spirituality all rose beyond their own power in the decisive attitude of Christ, so that the question for the Christian, also today, is not how to make a synthesis of a human form of spirituality with the Christian one but how to master the human situation in the Spirit of Christ. The application of the norms of the Gospel to the human—and *a fortiori,* the ecclesiastical— forms of spirituality does not come from without but from within. The relating of everything to the divine Idea (in the Platonic *eros*), the shaping of man's instinctive and subjective existence through objective understanding and commitment (in the *praxis* and *hexis* of Aristotle), the surrender to the absolute Logos in spite of all objections of finite reason (in the *apatheia* of the Stoa)—all these are inwardly transcended in Christ's love for the Father in the Spirit. Thus, if the modern man is a Christian, all that his anonymous service of the world needs is a deeper penetration into the ultimate selflessness of Jesus, the Servant of God and man, in order to attain with him the ultimate freedom.

Albert-Marie Besnard, O.P./*Saulchoir, France*

Tendencies of Contemporary Spirituality

Everything leads us to think that new forms of spirituality are taking shape in contemporary Catholicism. The rapid evolution of our society has brought profound changes in the consciousness that each one has of his own mystery, of the collective destiny that sweeps him along and the universe that surrounds him. This fundamental consciousness constitutes the starting point, the elemental center that develops into a coherent and solid spirituality under the radiance of a lively faith. Changes in this fundamental consciousness call forth profound changes in the spirituality of the men of our time.

The manner in which faith penetrates and transforms this human principle depends in turn on the particular awareness that Christians have of the Gospel preached to them, which they are to live and to which they must bear witness. But here again the Council has prepared and is carrying out such a revival of the spirit of the Gospels among the faithful, that one might speak of a rediscovery of even the most traditional sources of spirituality.

Moreover, the element of rediscovery is all the more evident because new members of the faithful are showing for the first time a desire for an authentic spirituality. It is noticeable among militant people of all classes, who, as earnest witnesses of their faith, find themselves drawn toward spiritual challenges they never suspected. It is particularly noticeable also among those who are affected by their own witness and who discover or rediscover the Gospel in all its original strength. Spirituality is no longer the glorious ornament of a privileged lineage (clerical or bourgeois monastic families) who, because of ancient or recent traditions, have practiced it until now; it now springs up from nowhere, among Christians who owe their spiritual appetite to the Gospel and not to schools or centers of spirituality which they usually ignore entirely.

It is one thing to suspect the existence of a new spirituality and another to trace its distinctive shape. It is easier to write a history of spirituality than to make a forecast. For one thing, it is difficult to discern among the tendencies of the moment those that are ephemeral and those that are deep enough to serve as a lasting basis for the spirituality of the new generation. In spirituality as in other things there are styles, passing fads that are translated into catchwords, slogans, best-sellers; after a few years they are cast aside as vigorously as they had previously been acclaimed. These short-lived enthusiasms are certainly not without significance in studying the spirituality of a period, but while they have a place in history, they are misleading as immediate pastoral guides.

There is another reason for uncertainty in tracing the spirituality that is now evolving. When one speaks of spirituality, one refers to a living synthesis of human and evangelical elements. Spirituality is really the structuring of an adult personality in faith according to one's proper genius, vocation and charismatic gifts, on the one hand, and according to the laws of the universal Christian mystery on the other. Now these given elements are so rich and varied (and some are still in flux) that one can scarcely foresee the result of a synthesis: in fact, several syntheses are possible. Should we use the term "postconciliar spirituality"? Should we speak instead of spiritualities so diverse as to become ecclesial communities within the bosom of a catholicity that agrees to accept the rights of legitimate differences and particular situations within the one People of God?

Such are the considerations urging us to present a few modest statements that may serve as points of departure for deeper and more precise considerations.

I

The Increasing Need for Spirituality Today

We have already mentioned that the desire for spirituality has been felt by new members of the faithful. This is a noteworthy fact that might have been predicted once Christian people found again the true source and meaning of their faith. In fact, he who enters or reenters the faith, from the outset, from the time when he is first taught about Christ, must continue on to "things more perfect" (Heb. 6, 1), which, as St. Paul shows clearly, is by no means a luxury reserved for the few, but rather the normal development of mature faith (1 Cor. 2). The fact is more remarkable when we notice that Christians, who began by the rediscovery of the apostolate, the Christian meaning of human work, or the Gospel and the Bible, had also begun by rejecting all that resembled the spirituality and piety they had previously been taught. However, these same people, as they develop, enriched by their Christian experience and by trying to interpret its message (for they have been purified in many ways: by activity, trials of faith, unexpected graces, different ecclesial fellowships), realize little by little that they need a spirituality, what St. Paul calls "the wisdom of God", and that they need spiritual guides to teach them. Judging by these requests, which are more and more frequent and in line with the very obvious evolution of the present time, perhaps it is time to make known that, after the revitalization of the pastoral office through what is called "pastoral theology", a rediscovery of its spiritual function is in order through what we shall have to call a "spiritual theology".

However, one must guard against premature enthusiasm. If St. Paul lamented that the faithful in Corinth were slow in attaining spiritual wisdom (1 Cor. 3, 1-2), he also had to call a halt to the spiritual speculation that deviated from the Gospel in the

Churches of Asia Minor, especially at Colossus (Col. 2). Here and there we hear of requests for a "theory" of spirituality that seem questionable. In some cases they indicate a genuine desire for entering into a fuller experience of the evangelical life by deepening and interiorizing it. In other cases one cannot be sure whether or not they are expressing the weakness of a religious spirit which, discouraged by confrontation with the world and disturbed by threats presented by an environment of unbelief, would prefer to withdraw into a protected circle for "spiritual dialogue" or spiritual retreats.

As long as one limits oneself to spirituality, one is safe: certain grave problems of the world and of the faith will not be brought up. Why waste one's time and strength trying to figure out the way to the kingdom of God in the confusion and darkness of a society bogged down in the temporal, the concerns of politics, economics, and technology? Let us lift our souls above these troubling entanglements, and let us speak among ourselves about God, biblical commentaries, meditation, yoga! We've had enough talk about action, witnessing, transforming society, fighting for justice or for peace: we are men of the purely spiritual, clear and unchanging doctrine; we contemn the world. This same questionable attitude is found among the laity in regard to the priestly ministry, when they ask their priests to give them God and nothing more, and to confine themselves to their spiritual ministry. We can rightly ask ourselves what God, what spirituality are they referring to? Using formulas that can have a legitimate meaning, they can be aiming at something not in the spirit of the Gospel.

Here we see the fundamental dilemma of spirituality. On the one hand, we conceive of it as the search for refined religiosity that is lived for its own sake, the doctrines of which may be correct in theory, but which betray their emptiness by diverting us from an integral Christian life and by distorting history and genuine personal commitment. At this point spirituality becomes synonymous with idealism along religious lines and, when carried to its logical conclusion, it fringes on gnosticism. On the other hand, spirituality may mean something *lived* in a most personal, serious way—the integral life that faith in Jesus Christ gives us as we live in *this* century, among *these* men, in *this* world. Obviously it is in this latter sense that we use the term "spirituality" and that we take an interest in it.

One may divide the essential tendencies that characterize present-day spirituality into three headings (corresponding to the three dimensions of any spirituality: the context of the world of men in which it is expressed; the person who lives it; the church that is its special milieu): it is a spirituality that takes as its starting point life lived in the world we know; it is a spirituality that aspires to real, personal experience; lastly, it is a spirituality that repudiates individualism and tends to thrive in small fraternal associations.

II

A SPIRITUALITY FOR LIFE IN THE WORLD

Necessarily then, the spirituality sought by the Christian today is above all a spirituality to be lived. A spiritual doctrine interests him only if it offers the means to better give himself to God and to better organize the substance of his daily life in the name of the Lord. People will speak of a spirituality of marriage, a spirituality of work, a spirituality of events and human relations, a spirituality of leisure, etc. One must take care not to be misled. We are not talking about coloring our actions with a spiritual purpose which, missing the real meaning of these actions, would not penetrate them from beginning to end and which would content itself with sprinkling them with a pious and ineffectual blessing. Christians today are well aware that spiritualizing their life does not mean having a vague mental advertence to God in the intervals between their professional duties or vital concerns, nor injecting some elevation of soul into their spare time. This would be the spirituality that they originally rejected! No, it is the very stuff of existence that must acquire a new quality in its very depths, a quality that enables it to be ever more and more the matter and the form of the kingdom of God.

It is perhaps well to note that the instinctive desire expressed here is not limited to Christians. To give a spiritual and profound meaning to one's life, taking life as it is and not distorting it, to bestow an interiority that is not a psychological coating, not an inconsistent superstructure, but rather a spirituality that is interior, that expands one's personality into all the human space that it is one's vocation to fill: such is the desire of man as man when he reaches a certain level of consciousness and dignity. In spite of dramatic conflicts and unknown factors, which make the actual development of humanity unpredictable, man's progress is so marked in many respects that thoughtful and right thinking people recognize that man is truly becoming more noble, and they draw from this a personal and undeniable nobility of soul.

It is not astonishing that unbelievers go as far as they do in the pursuit of spirituality; Christian apologetics would do well not to consider the "spiritualization" of the human condition as a sufficient criterion of the truth of a religion or as a monopoly of Christianity. If we agree first of all to understand the word "spirituality" as fundamental harmony, the destiny of the spirit which is in man, let us openly acknowledge that not only non-Christian but also non-believing systems of spirituality can and will exist.

The believer should not be troubled in discovering this. His own spirituality is precisely what it is because the destiny of his own mind was seized upon, saved, enlarged to the point of participating in the mystery of God himself, thanks to the Holy Spirit that has been given him. But the distinctively new thing about Christianity, the Christian miracle, is this: it is through all his human fullness that the believer penetrates the fullness of God (cf. Eph. 3, 19). In order to approach God, in order to offer him spiritual worship, the Christian is not supposed to forget, still less deny, what makes up his existence and his earthly destiny: it is his very way of life that is the matter of his spiritual sacrifice; it is his actions, his loves, his sufferings that make up the themes of his debate with God, of that endless and dramatic "encounter" with God that spells out his destiny.

The language with which God speaks to man and man to God is not primarily words, but rather daily events, those choices that souls are continually called to make because of their very existence, and which the Incarnation has shown us as not only the life of man, but the life of Christ in man, and yet no less the life of Christ. This language is of course difficult to decipher and still more difficult to speak! Present-day Christians have the courage to understand that they must not seek for any other language; this has been true since Abraham first heard the voice of God. In this, perhaps, lies the secret of the surprising openness of the contemporary believer with regard to this Word of God and the Bible. He hears in it a God who is calling to man in the center of his environment and in his human tasks; he understands that there is no spirituality without knowing how to answer such a call with one's whole being.

The spirituality of the non-sacred, the spirituality of terrestrial realities, the spirituality of human values: under a thousand names and by a thousand paths, this is the only spirituality that is sought. But such seeking involves a risk that should not be underestimated. One way of insisting that the encounter with God takes place within the context of our daily life, and not outside it, ends by reducing this encounter to nothing more than the experience of daily existence. Christian spirituality would then be no different than the spiritualization to which, as we said, an unbeliever can attain, except perhaps that the unbeliever cannot identify an experience fixed in anonymity.

People are so aware that the living God is manifested in the ordinary course of things, without upsetting the process but with an overall integration of the world in salvation history, that certain minds might experience difficulty in thinking about the divine transcendence and in entering into relations of spirit to Spirit and person to Person with the God of Jesus Christ. Such relations may be distinct and eventually disconnected from the con-

comitant relations with others or with the world. That God is at
work in all things, that in this redeemed world the free choice of
the good on the part of any man represents an implicit option
for Christ until the latter is made known to him, that we shall be
judged by the effective love that we show to one another: these
are truths often heard before. However, a certain way of repre-
senting them to ourselves and of living them might easily lead to
a confusion of the plans of men with the designs of God, of totally "immanentizing" the action of God in the works of men.
On the spiritual plane, the most visible symptom of this devia-
tion is the inevitable damage done to the contemplative dimension of the Christian mystery; this becomes devitalized at the
root by the conviction that it is really nothing but a useless, although beautiful, aberration of the soul.

In our opinion such tendencies stem above all from the difficulties of reconciling with theological orthodoxy those insights
of a very new and very rich experience, rather than from a latent
heresy. They reveal a mistake rather than the mistakenness of an
effort which aims at giving form and an answer to questions that
our generation asks in different and intensely serious terms (for
example, the relations between the development of humanity and
the kingdom of God; or between secular history and salvation
history; the precise implications for Christians of the laicization
of society, or rather of the disappearance of the religious sense in
the masses; the mode of Christ's presence among those who,
while not knowing him, yet seem to live according to values that
are almost evangelical, etc.). All this must alert theologians to
the urgent need for a spirituality that can answer these questions
and provide the means of plunging into the heart of faith instead
of remaining outside. The stakes are high indeed.

III

A SPIRITUALITY OF EVANGELICAL EXPERIENCE

We have used the word "experience". Though at first sight it
may seem ambiguous, it characterizes a fundamental tendency

of present-day spirituality. We shall try to explain this as clearly as possible, hoping to avoid extravagant theories.

Modern man is subjected to a constant stimulation of the senses. He is invited to see, hear, touch and taste things more and more. Though sometimes frightened at this absurd and reckless waste, we understand, too, the extraordinary and irreversible course of our journey. The world with its infinite possibilities is being increasingly confronted, conquered, and surrendered to man who can embrace and grasp a thousand treasures formerly unheard of or only dreamed about. "Living" in the fullest sense of the word, so that our eyes sparkle with desire, may of course mean artificial stimulation, exhausting ourselves in the anarchic accumulation of sensations, knowledge, encounters; but it may also mean developing and expressing our personalities, thanks to contacts with meaningful realities and most humanizing experiences. As part of a stupendous universe to which he has the vocation of giving a meaning in order to dicover his own meaning, man moves across the world, which envelops and bathes him on all sides, with wonder, wildness and delight; or else he struggles against its limitations with fierceness, pain and hope. He creates a sphere of civilization where the intensity of life becomes a decisive variable that constantly increases; once he has tasted it, he can no longer be interested in, or believe, anything that would decrease this variable. This intensity of life represents at the same time a dangerous adventure; human destiny takes on such direction and proportions that ancient wisdom seems outmoded; by his business with the world, man sows his own mind with questions of unending number and seriousness.

Since the task of a Christian is to give an evangelical direction to his life and to participate in the world without ceasing to participate in God through Christ, he will seek the key to this difficult situation in his spiritual life. It, too, must be fitted into a program of "intensity of life". He needs to test by experience its lights, its helps, its nourishment. God must remain God for him, the God who is greater than all (than all the things he discovers) and nearer than all (than all the things which press upon him).

The Word of God must remain an effective Word in all the questions he asks himself and in the darkness through which he passes. Prayer must take on an earnestness and a meaning that is all the more serious in that it seems useless and more futile to the modern soul.

These are the terms in which a Christian expresses his requirements for a renewed Christian experience. He is not seeking experience for the sake of experience, feeling for the sake of feeling; it is not a sort of spiritual dilettantism added to the dilettantisms of all the other human "experiences" that he has the leisure to have, without any real involvement of his soul. He seeks to live by Christ in a universe that subjects him to terrible tensions and contradictory allurements; perhaps, we must admit, he is simply seeking to survive as a Christian.

Do not be tempted to denounce such an aspiration as a detestable product of the subjectivism of our day. A haunting fear of certain aberrations has made the term "religious experience" quite suspect; it is regrettable inasmuch as this suspicion may prevent us from detecting the true aims of the modern Christian, which are not really those of romanticism or individualistic subjectivism. Very fortunately, theology is concerned once more with clarifying a problem that is as old as Christianity.[1] It is sufficient, in fact, to study the faith of the primitive Church and to look over the history and forms of spirituality to be convinced that it has always been, in the last analysis, the proof and special manifestation of what must be called the Christian experience. To refuse to recognize this term and what it stands for would be to open oneself to ridicule and confusion, and at the same time to prove that one has not the least idea of what an authentic spiritual life is. History teaches us as well that the most arduous task of spiritual people in all times has been to distinguish between true and false experience; there is no area more difficult to handle than this. The dangers of spiritual pleasure-seeking, religious

---

[1] J. Mouroux, *The Christian Experience* (Sheed and Ward, 1954). M. Dupuy, "Experience spirituelle et théologie comme science," in *Nouvelle Revue Théologique* (December, 1964), pp. 1137f.

estheticism and uncontrolled subjectivism are not always too different from certain ways of satisfying our sensibility. But to eliminate the need for discerning by merely suppressing the subject is not a solution that is wise or lasting. One must be resigned to the fact that this spiritual renewal is full of risks. Or rather, one must make up one's mind that, in a world full of risks, the Gospel can thrive.

Christians who, under the impulse of the Holy Spirit, devote themselves to this continuation of the Gospel have begun to make an astonishing discovery (the most astonishing thing is that it has come to the point of being astonishing): there are in the authentic treasures of the Church and in its living tradition more insights, more resources, more help than is needed to face victoriously (with that victory that is our faith; cf. 1 John 5, 4) the world that is taking shape around us. Do not read the history of the present-day renewal in the Church as if it were the fruit of considerations conducted with order, deductive reasoning and tranquillity. The renewal has sprung from the pressure of an irresistible need. The spiritual impotence to which an anemic and antiquated piety reduced them, forced militant and convinced Christians to seek a new spirituality in order to survive. They needed nothing other than the living and burning Word of God; they needed a liturgy that was a real encounter in mystery of the People of God (they themselves) with the living God who is their God. Theologians and pastors who have worked for these renewals have acted (more or less unconsciously) in order to answer these needs, which were at first unformulated, but became invested with a form that was more and more distinct and more and more exacting. The Holy Spirit has worked on the People of God, in the persons of its elect or of its "first fruits" who represent them; he has reopened for them the rivers of living water so that, in the new desert of unbelief in the world, they might not die of dryness and thirst. Consequently, we have retrieved some theological and spiritual currents, which because of the vicissitudes of history especially during the Counter-Reformation were no longer offering their life-giving waters to Catho-

lics (the meaning of the Word of God, the universal priesthood
of the faithful, etc.). In this context one can see why the present
Council is likely to have profound repercussions on spirituality
that are as yet unpredictable.

The point that interests us particularly has one reassuring aspect. If Christians today want a spirituality that is a truly personal experience, they want to get it from authentic sources.
They care little for experiencing sublime sentiments that might
not be guaranteed by what is most solid in our faith. At least
these are the Christians who will bring about the spiritual renewal. Is it not at the sources that it is most legitimate to experience "how good the Lord is" (Ps. 34, 9)? For example, is not
the liturgy the ecclesial milieu par excellence of the Christian experience, and will it not become increasingly so in a way that is
more and more real for the faithful of our day? Does not the
Bible, read in the analogical way of faith and in accord with an
uninterrupted tradition of *lectio divina,* permit us to "savor the
good word of God" (Heb. 6, 5)? This return to the sources is a
good sign. Of course it will not guarantee of itself that spiritual
experience is what it should be, but it does have the advantage of
ridding us, from the start, of a certain number of pathological
forms of religious experience (excessive sentimentality, unbal-
anced devotions, gnoses of all sorts, etc.). It does not prevent us
from being able to misuse the Bible as well as the liturgy. However, it offers better bases for spiritual maturity and it is more
controlled by the Church than any other spiritual movement.

A vigorous Christian experience is required as a valid answer
and as a nourishing substance in the midst of the questions and
trials that faith undergoes at present. This requirement can also
be expressed, and this is what we should like to emphasize, in
terms of "evangelism". In fact, there is no spiritual awakening
without a resurgence of evangelism and vice versa. Indeed, since
we are not about to procure the luxury of a new spirituality
merely for the sake of something new, but rather to live with
truth today the Gospel of all days, the realization of the Gospel
becomes the special object of our spiritual quest. Inversely, if

evangelism has as its dynamism the astounding allurement of the beatitudes; if it is based on the conviction, the certitude, that a real poverty, a real simplicity, a true fraternity can transform the world; if it has for its supreme intention the desire of obtaining free access to the Father, a filial familiarity with God, these are the first fruits of the Holy Spirit and the heart of the message of Jesus. Ardent present-day Christians are longing to speak of Jesus Christ and of the infinite condescension of God and of communion in the Holy Spirit. They long to be effectively "evangelized", that is, to know the Good News for what it truly is: the proclamation and true appearance of joy and salvation from God.

They are in haste to be able to live the life of the kingdom. In this way they are renewing the old theme of the imitation of Christ by emphasizing Nazareth and its realization in daily life today. They are sensitive to the call, if not the difficult reality of poverty; they inquire anew about evangelical meekness in a world in which violence reigns, as well as vague and terrible threats of war.

With all that we have said on this subject, the characteristic note of evangelism remains a lively preoccupation to be effective. This means that the truth of Christianity will be demonstrated for the most part by its capacity to transform men; this transformation is essentially a change of heart, one that is more fitted for attacking the great problems of the space age. Many unbelievers, and even doubting believers, like to ask this question: what is changed when one becomes a Christian? They do not ask what change there is in the simple and incommunicable vision of the Christian's mind, but in his conduct, his action, his control of situations and events. One can be sure that solid believers also ask themselves this, and that they expect from spirituality some light and answers on this point. They have a right to expect them, because the Gospel really requires them to be the "light of the world" and because their good works are the sign of the salvation that comes from God (cf. Matt. 5, 16).

Perhaps this will provide the occasion for the contemporary

Christian to relearn some of the spiritual laws that he failed to recognize through impatience or ignorance. Eager to transfer his efficiency as an apostolic man to the visible course of history, and deceived by the seductions of a technical sort of efficiency, he forgets the condition necessary for spiritual efficiency: long, hard work on oneself, which empowers the disciple of the Gospel to witness authentically as a "new man". He likes to think that it is enough to love; and in this he is not wrong, but he may not always suspect the price that must be paid to love like Jesus Christ In other words, he needs to rediscover an asceticism for which he hardly suspects any use.

In the same vein, his legitimate desire to live a coherent Christian life, which will effect a noticeable modification of his conduct and actions, forces him sometimes into dubious, simplistic and ineffectual theories. Wanting at all costs to experience his Christianity and the influence of faith on his existence, he forgets that the life of Christ in us is not confined to what we feel or to what is shown outwardly. The divine action penetrates the depths where our consciousness cannot penetrate, and it animates our existence by light impulses which our exterior acts are not always capable of interpreting. In many types of banal activities, in the social or technical domain, there is no place for an emergence of the faith as such; a Christian is not outwardly distinguished from a non-Christian when he manipulates his tools or when he goes from one window to another filling out blanks for administrative purposes. Yet it is not true that there are several sections in his life that are totally extrinsic to each other. His activities as "Mr. So-and-so" in society, as an anonymous consumer and automatic producer, are not foreign to his spiritual life; but this is not to be understood in the simplistic fashion sometimes imagined. This is still another point that must be remedied by present-day spirituality.

IV

A Spirituality Lived in Evangelical Brotherhood

One last characteristic worthy of notice in the spirituality which is being worked out, and which distinguishes it from its immediate predecessors, is the instinctive rejection of all individualism. In seeking a spiritual life, Christians will often firmly refuse to pursue solitary paths. They are all eager to find or to form a group whose ambiance and objectives correspond to their aspirations and needs. These groups appear with a structure more or less clearly defined ranging anywhere from occasional and ephemeral groups to genuine secular institutes, while in between can be found all sorts of associations and movements that are encouraged or simply approved. This very proliferation is an indication of a deep current that is quite remarkable.

In a sense this is nothing new. Just as in profane history, there has often been a tendency in the history of spirituality for restriction to charismatic personalities who by their actions, their doctrine and their writings have attained a particular prominence among us. But, as soon as one looks more closely at the socio-religious context in which these personalities appeared, one notices at once not only that they are inseparable from the spiritual currents that favored their birth (think of the ferment of evangelism in the 13th century which was the incubator of St. Francis of Assisi and St. Dominic), but that they are organically linked to the communities which played an important role as midwives or stimulants of their spiritual doctrine: for instance, the "famiglia" grouped around Catherine of Siena, the "brothers and sisters of the common life" who at the end of the 14th century developed the "devotio moderna", the reformed communities of Carmel in the 16th century around Teresa of Avila and John of the Cross, etc. Conventicles, clubs, groups, brotherhoods, and other communitarian cells seem to be a constant phenomenon of the sociology of spirituality.

This phenomenon, of course, produces great diversity of objectives. Hence, the "brothers and sisters of the common life" cultivated a spirituality only partially responsible for the individualism that has had such a baneful effect on Catholic piety of the last centuries. We ought to show precisely how the conditions that always, or at least frequently, produce a spiritual impetus in the Church actually exist today in a new context. To begin with, certain all-important facts about the mentality of contemporary man point up and develop the picture. The new dimensions of man's solidarity, the closer interweaving of human lives by the socialism of everyday existence, the custom of working in teams as an absolute necessity for a successful enterprise, the latent anxiety of the individual with regard to a dreaded solitude without affection: all these are needs consciously felt which, as indications of the strength or the weakness proper to man in our day, tend forcibly and legitimately to influence the form of spiritual life. The interdependence of individuals has never been so complex and widespread. More and more the keys to the projects of each one are in part in the hands of others. This is obvious with regard to the self-realization of man's Christian being.

The lived realization of these facts has probably played a large role in the revival of the communitarian values of Christianity. If the socializing tendencies of the modern world entail disturbing risks, Christians have suddenly become aware that they can also give a new body to values fully in accord with those of the Gospel. In addition, the best way of avoiding the extravagances and aberrations of certain collectivisms is to make known how the spirit of Christ, by its hidden and special role in the human race, makes the individual more of a person, whom it inserts into a network of most intense relations and most intimate communion. It was not possible for Christianity to be deprived of a good that was its very own, not that it be paradoxically excluded from aspiring to it. Christianity alone can give collectivity its true sense; and community spirit is necessary for Christianity to preserve its meaning.

When the time comes to write the history of present-day

spirituality, we can be certain that this discovery will be one of the most significant of our century. Such a history might show how a renewed interest arose, at first obscure and vague, then more conscious and distinct, in the doctrine of the Mystical Body. The Encyclical of Pius XII appeared in 1943, and it is certainly a significant date; but the doctrine might not have reappeared unless the spirituality of that time required its lights, and one would need to go much further back to find the origins of this revival. It might be noted here that the liturgical renewal has become inseparable from the communitarian or social dimension of the liturgy; it may be said that the slow maturation culminates in the pastoral and theological exposition of the mystery of the "assembly". The apostolic impetus, at first operative in Catholic Action among the laity, then by the more and more insistent concern for a concerted pastoral effort among the clergy, now begins to give an accepted status in the Church to the idea and actual working of a *team*. The whole Church is finding again a keen sensibility toward what is its very essence: a communion in Christ and in the Spirit, on all levels where this mystery is manifest. The fact that the Council has preferred the theological term "People of God" and that the collegial structure of the hierarchy has been brought to public notice are examples at the summit of this tendency which marks a beginning as well as an end. The same is true in the lower ranks where all sorts of groups are coming together for the furtherance of the evangelical or the spiritual life.

These groups fulfill several functions, not always clearly envisaged by their members. The first would concern the practice of the evangelical life. Some Christians, seeking to carry out their evangelical aspirations, feel the crying need of a community where they will be able to realize certain great values of the Gospel, such as were shown by the primitive community in Jerusalem. They want, as they say, to "incarnate" these values, to render them tangible; they are not to be satisfied with talking about them, but in living them. They instinctively understand that the community is the Gospel made visible. A shared life, modest perhaps but real; a fraternal communion which has an inner structure of human friendship that is quite palpable; a prayer which, in order to be the prayer of several people, does not cease to be the prayer of each one: here are the many requirements that seek satisfaction in the new groups, necessarily and vitally linked to, but not identifiable with, the associations of their local churches.

Another function of these groups is more concerned with apostolic life. If the community is the Gospel made visible, it is therefore also a witness for a world which has mistaken ideas or knows nothing of this Gospel. Solitude and mission, it seems more and more evident, are of necessity mutually exclusive. The missionary pioneers deliberately choose to put themselves in teams or brotherly associations, but there are also mere laymen who want to witness to their faith in their milieux. In such groups certain circumstances readily communicate spiritual values: diverse and complementary charisms, the stimulation of the faith by dialogue among members of the team, mutual correction by the practice of "revision of life", etc. All this is at first lived from day to day without any pretension of elaborating spiritual doctrines; but when a team looks over the path that has been traveled, its members become aware that they are living a new brand of spirituality and that their evangelism is developing a new structure which is quite similar, but not identical, to what one finds in the great periods of traditional spirituality. One can predict that in spirituality, as in other areas of the life of the Church, apostolic and missionary communities will play leading roles that are very worthwhile.

In a non-believing society all these groups can furnish indispensable supply lines. Fundamental atheism, which today has a more and more firmly established position, brings to Christians the duty not to take refuge in ghettos or well-fortified citadels, but rather to be firmly convinced that they are Christians-together, united by a very palpable brotherhood. Instinctively they begin to establish centers where each one can lean on the faith of the other: places where it is "good for brethren to live together" (Ps. 133, 1), where they can be strengthened in unanimity before scattering for that difficult evangelical fidelity in the world, centers where the Lord is present in the midst of those assembled in his name (Matt. 18, 20). This desire in its overall impulse is legitimate. It is quite normal for believers to desire to "experience the comforting" presence of others who share their faith (cf. Rom. 1, 12). They are well aware of the trials that lie in wait for them at one time or another: doubt, weariness, the burden of the questions that the world presents to them. At such times they need brethren near at hand to become for them persuasive witnesses to the Lord; and he who comes to the help of his brother may easily be the one who needs support himself the next day.

These new groups may obviously go off the correct path. It is only too easy to turn into a kind of sect or chapel, a spiritual fraternity that would cease to be a faithful and true manifestation of the "Ecclesia" under the humble guise of an "ecclesiola" authorized by the hierarchy. The latter will often experience the fear that the multiplying of groups scatters energies to the detriment of the Church's central mission in the world. There is also the danger that the faithful might go off to seek in these new communities what they should have found in the existing structural communities in churches and parishes; but it is well known that there are real problems here that are not solely due to the gigantic size of certain local churches. It is surely true that communities with particular spiritual needs have no rightful meaning unless they constitute relay groups who offer relief to the larger assemblies of the local churches and their normal organizations. They must actualize the ecclesial mystery without reducing it to shreds or overburdening it. In the long run they can do no more than be of service to the liturgical, charitable and apostolic life of the Church. But it is no easier for a group than it is for an individual to serve wholeheartedly a more universal communion. We cannot fail to recognize that the modern phenomenon of smaller associations, while it reveals an authentic seeking of the common good, also involves a decidedly defensive attitude with regard to society, which they consider too all-encompassing and too anonymous. One discovers a sort of group individualism which is just as fatal to the true communal spirit as the individualism of individuals. Some men, of course, may form associations not so much to initiate an experience of community that will draw them nearer and nearer (and later result in a communion that is more and more extensive) as to collectively protect themselves against the temptation of opening outward, which really frightens them. Spiritual associations do not escape this risk. Even the fraternity that is most balanced at the outset, both evangelically and ecclesiologically, can end up, if one is not careful, by being faithful to the Spirit in the name of a spirituality that has gone sour. What can one say about groups which from the outset were formed more or less deliberately to escape from the deepest movements that carry the Church along toward its missionary future among men?

This could be the general conclusion of our study. Spiritual movements indicate unmistakably the vitality of the Church; for this reason we can only hope for and favor their development. But they are also the most delicate and vulnerable flowerings of life in the Church; all sorts of maladies can afflict them. It would be a grave error on the part of pastors and theologians to be aloof to their needs and their objectives. The advice that St. Paul gives is always pertinent: "Do not extinguish the Spirit, do not undervalue the gifts of prophecy, but test everything; what is good, keep it" (1 Thess. 5, 19-20).

François Vandenbroucke, O.S.B./*Louvain, Belgium*

Spirituality and Spiritualities

Christians today are more keenly aware than ever before of the number of spiritualities in the Church.[1] Communication is frequent among different levels of Christianity, different social classes and different religious orders, each springing from a special tradition. Christians of the East are meeting Christians from the West. Catholics are contacting Protestants, reviewing the spiritual heritage they have drawn from the Bible and the liturgy, and comparing their traditions with traditions derived elsewhere.

There is reason to rejoice over these many forms of spiritualities. In a certain sense they are a sign of the Lord's manifold gifts. Yet it is important to look at these spiritual traditions as they really are, without exaggeration or distortion. Is there reason to lament over this situation? Yes, inasmuch as they raise barriers and make it difficult for Christians, and even for

---

[1] Rather than burden the text with cumbersome footnotes, it has seemed preferable to present a short bibliography:

L. Bouyer, J. LeClercq, F. Vandenbroucke, L. Cognet, *Histoire de la Spiritualité chrétienne*, 3 Vols. (Paris, 1960-61); C. Butler, *Ways of Christian Life* (London, 1932); J. De Guibert, *Leçons de théologie spirituelle* (Toulouse, 1946), pp. 108-22; L. De Saint-Joseph, "Ecoles de spiritualité," in *Dict. Spir.* IV, vols. 115-28; J. Gautier, ed. *Some Schools of Catholic Spirituality* (New York, 1959); L. Genicot, *La Spiritualité médiévale* (Je sais, je crois: Paris, 1958); G. Thils, *Sainteté chrétienne* (Tielt, 1958), pp. 535-63; *Le scuole cattoliche di spiritualità* (Milan, 1945).

Catholics, of the same country, the same culture and the same social milieu to understand one another. It would be still more serious if this situation were to lead to real schisms or heresies in the Church.

The trend at the present moment is to deplore the multiplication of spiritualities. Yet this is inevitable to some extent even in the East where different schools of spirituality do not exist but where neighboring traditions are sharply defined. In the West it is not rare to find great spiritual leaders who come from the same background, who share the same civilization, who stress doctrines that are basically the same but who are stamped with their own particular point of view. Take, for example, Teresa of Avila, Ignatius Loyola and John of the Cross. They were practically contemporaries in 16th-century Spain. They were fired with the same apostolic zeal to serve the Church and each attained a high degree of mystical life. Yet how different are these heroes of sanctity in temperament and in personal vocation.

Take another example. A group of highly spiritual Dominicans lived in close proximity in the Rhine valley in 14th-century Germany: Master Eckhardt, John Tauler and Henry Suso. The first was consumed by a dialectic thirst and refused to be satisfied with words when preaching. This raised doubts about his orthodoxy. John Tauler was more like John of the Cross and insisted on the practice of abnegation in order to reach mystical union. Henry Suso was more restrained than the other two, resembling a knight in love with the wisdom that comes from Christ.

About the same time and not far away in the southern part of the region now known as the Low Countries, lived the great Brabant mystic, John Ruysbroeck. In spite of very different choices, in spite of obviously dissimilar temperaments, each of these mystics was seeking practically the same ideal: to allow the Word to be born in the soul and, as preparation for this birth, to open himself to all the exigencies of radical abnegation.

If, among men closely related in time and space, we find these great differences that can be explained primarily in terms of temperament and milieu, how much more pronounced will be these differences in comparing men who lived in different lands and centuries apart. A parallel may be found in different artistic, scientific, philosophic, theological, and even economic, political or social schools. It is indeed a fact of human existence.

Where does this multiplicity begin? What are its causes? First of all, we should recall the fact of divine providence and have trust in its designs. At certain critical periods in the history of the Church, powerful personalities have been raised up, and these personalities themselves realized that they were conditioned, so to speak, by their environment. In all this we should see the normal and legitimate working of providence which uses human instruments to hasten the coming of God's kingdom.

But we must probe more deeply into the problem of the causes of this multiplicity. For example, what separates the Rhenish school mentioned above from the Dutch school that rose in the wake of John Ruysbroeck? What separates the Dominican school from the Franciscan school? More concretely, what separates Dominic from Francis of Assisi and Thomas Aquinas from Bonaventure? One answer is the influence of strong personalities who were able to impress their mark on generations of disciples. This accounts for differences of psychology, temperament and character among the leaders as well as among their disciples. At the beginning of every school of spirituality can be found an original experience of one of these strong personalities and this experience is twofold: the experience of the founder's personal interior life and the experience of the effective spiritual formation of his first disciples.

Both of these experiences may not have been equally successful. In the case of Francis of Assisi, for example, the second experience, that of the formation of his disciples, was certainly defective. On the other hand, the imitators may have been guilty of faults and omissions even in their spiritual life, and these may have had serious consequences, as was true in the case of the Dutchman, Gerard Groote (d. 1384) to whom may be traced the beginning of the spiritual trend of *Devotio moderna*. It may be useful to distinguish between these two experiences when forming a judgment about a school, or a religious order or a spiritual type. The second is more essential to the founding of a school than the first. Benedict Labre, for example, was destined to remain alone. In his case, there was no second experience; he had no disciples, he founded no school. On the contrary, Don Bosco succeeded in forming a large group prolonging his personal experience in spite of the inequalities and even the inadequacies of his disciples themselves. Dominic knew how to fix his own mark so strongly upon a group of disciples that his school continues to bear his name even to the present day. This is also true of Francis of Assisi, although many of his spiritual groups owe much to early disciples like Bonaventure.

Are powerful personalities the only explanation of the different forms of spirituality that exist in the Church? Interest should not be focused on great initiators alone. Authentic differences exist between different spiritual climates, different countries, different centuries. Occasionally, in the same country and at the same time, spiritual needs can vary with different levels of the population. For example, England was patently pragmatic in the 14th century, attaching relatively little importance to theoretical and even dogmatic questions. Its approach to religion was individualistic. Liturgy had little or no importance while the people themselves were more concerned about problems connected with subsistence, government and politics.

These characteristics can be noted in the works of Richard Rolle, Walter Hilton and the anonymous author of the admirable treatise, *The Cloud of Unknowing*.[2] At almost the same time there appeared on the Continent the *Devotio moderna,* a spiritual movement traceable to Gerard Groote and his disciples. Originally known as the Brothers of the Common Life, they soon became the Canons of Windesheim. Here a certain pessimism is dominant, characterized by a return to, and preaching

---

[2] *The Cloud of Unknowing and the Book of Privy Counselling* (edited from the manuscripts) (London: Oxford University Press, 1958).

of, the Gospel by means of an austere and intransigent asceticism. The atmosphere is clouded by the resignations and weaknesses of priests and religious, by the discords of the papacy and by the interminable conflicts of the Hundred Years' War.

Two centuries earlier in Western Europe, we also find general aspirations toward poverty and the Gospel in its purity. This movement characterizes the 12th and the beginning of the 13th century, apparently a popular reaction to a feudalism ill-adapted to new social situations. Francis of Assisi and Dominic have a place in this movement which can also be seen in monks like Stephen of Muret and Joachim of Flora—not to mention men whose doctrine was suspect like Arnauld of Brescia, the Humiliati of Lyons, John Valdes and many others.

Many things become clear when these two factors, personality and spiritual climate, are considered. But do these two factors explain everything? Prescinding from divine providence and the grace that inspires leaders, reformers and founders, it is probable, generally speaking, that these two factors do account for the different spiritualities that have appeared in the course of twenty Christian centuries.

It is sometimes alleged that the differing combinations of the great means of perfection explain the differences between two spiritualities. For example, Dominican spirituality is structured around preaching and theology; Franciscan spirituality, around the poverty of itinerant preachers. Or, we can say that monastic orders stress liturgical spirituality, the Carmelites accent mental prayer. Or again, the monastic orders, especially those of the Benedictine tradition, practice a poverty inspired both by Christ the worker in Nazareth and by the first Christians in Jerusalem who kept all their goods in common, while the Franciscans practice a poverty that resembles a type that springs from Bethlehem and Nazareth. In the Benedictine tradition, liturgical and biblical contemplation predominate, while in modern schools of spirituality, especially since the days of *Devotio moderna,* contemplation is more psychological, more subjective and devotional, even more saintly, centering around the great mysteries of Christ.

In its extreme form, modern spirituality comprises an elaborate technique of the methods of meditation and contemplation.

Furthermore, it should be noted that in the Church there are religious families that concentrate on one or another of Christ's mysteries. It is well known that the West during the first part of the Middle Ages centered its devotion on the most appealing mysteries of the life of Christ and Mary. Present-day aspirations to a rigorous poverty can be explained not only by the Marxist thought of our times, but also by accenting the Christ of the beatitudes.

Now these differen   , these various combinations, are always to be explained, as already noted, by the personalities of the initiators as well as by the spiritual climate, the human milieu, the sociological context. These give birth to spiritual types, "formulas", and, in the wake of great personalities, to true schools. Spiritualities are therefore the sum total of personalities and spiritual climates, characterized by a certain equilibrium among the various elements that are to be found in every Christian spirituality, such as asceticism, mental or mystical prayer, liturgical prayer and the practice of virtues.

What has just been said may be applied to the spirituality of a given social class, in the sense that this term is understood today. It may also be applied to the laity, clergy and religious. It is also possible to speak of a spirituality of the working class, of the rural class and of those engaged in the liberal professions, the technical world, social work, Catholic Action and many other fields.

But these types, these formulas, these schools evolve with mankind itself. What was created in the 13th century by Francis of Assisi and Dominic, while preserving certain traits that are the legacy of their personalities, continues to develop because mankind is in constant evolution. This means that there is no fixed school of spirituality. Today we cannot say that the Franciscan school is identically the same as it was in the 13th century. According to a frequently observed human law, this evolution follows a descending curve, marked by a decreasing spiritual tone that can be arrested only by new creators. The open religion of the heroes of whom Bergson spoke is always in danger of becoming closed, shut-in, sclerotic. Nevertheless, the principle of evolution is sound; it is the principle of the forward advance of man.

If the founders of a school or of an order, the men who created the atmosphere of their time and their milieu, could have anticipated or confronted the problems of later centuries, they would have met them in their own characteristic ways. It is the task of their successors to do today what the founders would do if they were here and not repeat the initial formula like slaves or robots. Such a repetition is disastrous; it is a negation of evolution. The Church can never be out of touch with the concrete, existential situation of man to which it offers itself and in which it lives.

All these considerations explain the multiplicity of spiritualities in the Church. We must now ask: What do all these schools of spirituality have in common? This brings us to the fundamental problem: What is *the* spirituality?

Spirituality is not the same thing as theology, especially dogmatic theology. The latter is a science that has the same object as faith itself, namely, revealed dogma, the Word of God. Spirituality is also, considered from an intellectual viewpoint, a science, "a methodically organized body of knowledge". But what is its object?

If we try to determine how the object of spirituality differs from that of theology, "the science of the revealed Word", the answer seems to be that spirituality has for its object "the reactions that the objects of faith raise in the religious conscience".[3] Every ascetical and mystical treatise studies the conduct of the soul vis-à-vis the data of revelation. Faith, hope, charity, virtues, gifts of the Holy Spirit, moral progress, vocal prayer and con-

---

[3] L. Bouyer, *La spiritualité du Nouveau Testament et des pères,* Vol. 1 of *Histoire de la spiritualité chrétienne* (Paris, 1960), p. 10. We depend here on remarks made by Fr. Bouyer about the frontiers of theology, morality and spirituality. All quotations following have been taken from his book. *See* Eng. Trans.: *Spirituality of the New Testament and the Fathers* (New York: Desclée, 1964).

templation are the different elements of the reacting spiritual organism.

Christian spirituality "does not hold the pseudo-scientific and altogether extravagant prejudice that the knowledge of objects polarizing the religious conscience must be basically foreign to the latter's knowledge. On the contrary, it studies them only in a living relation with them in a real understanding," as Newman puts it, "of what is believed".

Apparently it should be admitted that spirituality is not the same thing as morality or, more specifically, moral theology. This moral theology is also a science: the science of human acts, studied in the light of the Word of God. It includes, since it is a branch of theology, what revelation tells us about man's advance to God. It includes the consideration of Christian perfection, a perfection concretized in the Gospel. "Spirituality, however, concentrates on [those human acts] whose reference to God is not only explicit but immediate; that is, it is concerned above all with prayer and everything that is related to prayer in the ascetical and mystical life." In this, the character of explicit and immediate reference to God is absolutely essential.

In a word, spirituality is first of all the science of the reactions of the religious conscience vis-à-vis the object of faith—this is the intellectual aspect; secondly, it is the science of those human acts that have a special reference to God, that is, asceticism and mysticism. Thus, spirituality may be defined as the science of the application of the Gospel to Christian life on the intellectual plane, on the ascetical plane and on the properly mystical plane.

Let us say at once that this "application" has evolved in time and space. This is precisely why we can speak of schools, formulas and different types of spirituality—and, finally, of "spiritualities"; this is also why we can speak of a history of spirituality.

It is now possible to identify what is common to different Christian spiritualities, thereby clarifying what varies according to time and space. We have already discovered that "a" spirituality is a form of application of the Gospel to Christian life, and it is a way of realizing this application. However, it is not possi-

ble to distinguish these forms if an effort is not first made to establish what is common to all Christian spiritualities. Let us now
try to do this.

As we have said, priority in our considerations should be
given to the Gospel that controls the Christian's conduct. By the
Gospel we mean the Word of God addressed to man, bringing
man the wisdom of God, showing him how to go to God, opening before him the way that leads to God, offering him the means
of attaining eternal life. Secondly, we should never lose sight of
what can be explained by the general characteristics proper to all
men, whether of the 20th century, ancient times or the Middle
Ages, and whether or not they belong to different races; all have
much in common and, avoiding generalizations, exactly what
they have in common should be identified.

We should begin by discovering what truths in the Gospel are
absolutely valid always and everywhere, for every man and for
every Christian. This is no easy task. The Gospel itself was written at a definite moment in time in one specific place. Yet, it is
possible to reach something of a conclusion by laying down the
principle that the purpose of the divine message is to draw men
to union with God, to divinize them. Man is destined to become
the child of God and to live like a child of God. Let us say that
his "final cause" is to be oriented to God and that in this orientation he finds the fulfillment of his destiny.

We should also consider the model, "the exemplary cause",
that the Gospel proposes to every man, no matter who he may
be. This is not an abstract model, nor is it a code comparable
to Buddha's rules of wisdom. This model is a Person. Even when
this Person concretizes his teaching in certain simple precepts,
such as the eight beatitudes, the model for every Christian is still
a Person, Christ.

Since we are talking about causes that are operative in every
Christian spirituality, a word should be said about the efficient
cause of man's advance to God. This cause is also Christ. He is
the author of every grace, actual or habitual. Concretely, grace
obtains for us two things. First, of course, there is the negative

gift, the elimination of sin, the purification of the soul. The soul grows in the moral virtues. The soul grows in asceticism. This growth is possible only if the soul first strips itself of all that hinders its advance to God. Secondly, there is the positive gift, the grace that reestablishes or strengthens anew union with God through the theological virtues of faith, hope and charity. The development of these virtues constitutes an ascent whose end may be said to be mystical, in the sense that it leads to a certain insight into the truths of faith and the demands of a life lived according to these truths. Finally, it makes possible the presence of the Spirit in the soul.

These two elements, negative and positive, are complementary and equally necessary. For example, to forget the first would be to fall into angelism and a forgetfulness of the reality of the fall and redemption. This would lead to mysticism without asceticism and might result in some form of false illumination that has so often in the course of history disfigured the Church. On the contrary, to forget the second, the positive element, would mean descending into moralism. This would lead to the loveless practice of an asceticism that is without any mysticism or any profound awareness of the presence of God. This would be a spirituality of duty, a pure asceticism practiced in antiquity by sages such as Cicero who proposed a formula, admirable in itself but insufficient for a Christian, that was not measured to man's greatness.

In this connection we should recall the problems that the first generations of Christians had to face when confronted with the rationalistic civilization of pagan antiquity. A. J. Festingière, O.P., explains that this civilization was rationalistic because "evidently, thanks to reason, man has created both the arts that are necessary to life and the liberal arts; he has based the rules regulating his conduct on reason; he has applied himself to the disinterested study of all things according to the words of Cicero: *Ut omnia supera, infera, prima, ultima, media, videremus* (Tusc. 1:25:64)".[4]

[4] *Les Moines d'Orient I: Culture ou sainteté* (Paris, 1961), p. 14.

If Christians did not accept unquestioningly this limp and lifeless voluntaristic rationalism, which verges on stoicism, it was because they knew that such a perspective could never satisfy those who were seeking God and striving to live like children of God. It was not only a question of safeguarding a rhythm and a balance, in spite of the nobility that pagan antiquity succeeded in giving to the norms of human morality: "We, for our part, preach a crucified Christ—to the Jews indeed a stumbling-block and to the Gentiles foolishness, but to those who are called both Jews and Greeks, Christ, the power of God and the wisdom of God" (1 Cor. 1, 23-24).

Let us now consider, finally, the instrumental cause of every Christian spirituality. This cause is the Church with its hierarchy, sacraments and liturgy, Scripture and Tradition. This presupposes the acceptance of the principle of the ecclesiastical economy, without which it is impossible to speak of Christian spirituality except in the broad sense in which it is said that every grace comes through the Church, according to the formula *extra ecclesiam nulla salus* (outside the Church there is no salvation).

Usually, an authentic Christian spirituality develops "in the Church". But the meaning of membership in the Church, which was debated and clarified at Vatican Council II in connection with the Constitution on the Church and the Decree on Ecumenism, is fundamentally insertion in the divine filiation by baptism. It is in the logical prolongation of baptism that the mediation of those who come in the name of the Lord and of the successors of the apostles is accepted. This is why the different Christian spiritualities—Catholic, Protestant, Orthodox—can retain authentic elements of every Christian spirituality. Some treasures of the Christian message, but not all, have been channeled intact to these separate communities. Catholics should always remember that Protestant spirituality is basically baptismal and that Orthodox spirituality has never ceased to be episcopal and contemplative. While the former lacks the "succession" that Catholic hierarchy knows it has inherited from the apostles, the latter fails to acknowledge that the role of the bishop of Rome in the college of cardinals parallels that of Peter in the college of the apostles.[5] The ecumenical movement has reminded Catholics of these essential elements of Christian spirituality.

Let us point out that acceptance of the ecclesiastical economy is the minimum presupposed by every Catholic spirituality. When we speak of this acceptance, we do not mean anything like clericalism. We do mean the acceptance of those who have been sent by the Lord to carry his message, his good news, his Gospel.

It is worth noting that every Catholic spirituality of any importance has received a positive approbation from the Church, an approbation, however, that does not preserve it from deviations. It would be wrong to exaggerate the value of this approval. Its negative value is the affirmation that there is nothing contrary to Christian faith or customs in this spirituality. Its positive value is the authentication by the Church of a certain manner or type of application of the Gospel to Christian life.

It should also be observed that the Church usually takes as norms for such approbation the universal means of grace—the Bible, Tradition and the liturgy. As a matter of fact, every authentic Christian spirituality is biblical and liturgical because these two elements are integral to a living tradition.

In addition, what in us is everywhere and always, atemporal and permanent, must be identified. This anthropology can be made by examining the human being from the point of view of abstract philosophy with the help of truths from the rational psychology of the soul and its faculties. Care should be taken that, while we recognize what is common to all men, abstractly speaking, we should also observe that there are mentalities that differ widely because of social classes, races and individual endowments.

Modern psychology and sociology stress the importance of the individual and the collective situation in which asceticism and mysticism begin. These sciences help us to better understand the differences between spiritualities, or at least they enable us to

---

[5] Cf. *The Constitution on the Church*, Art. 22.

grasp their human unity. There is in fact, beyond these diversities, a unity that transcends all local and temporal indications. Paralleling in a certain sense the dogmatic tradition of the Church there is also a genuine experiential tradition; that is, there is throughout the whole of Christian history a continuity in the human reaction to the Gospel. Here again, Scripture, together with the impartial observation of events that have taken place in the last twenty centuries, provides some precise indications.

Everywhere and always the Christian soul feels the need of escaping from its fallen condition and situating itself on an absolute plane. This is the origin of the ascetical effort of conversion, the mystical effort of prayer and union with God which the Christian achieves by the practice of the theological virtues. This can also be discerned in today's *ersatz* religions—science, nuclear technology, spatial explorations—just as it could formerly be detected in magic, animism and naturism. Even Marxism does not escape from the human need to rise from a fallen condition to an absolute and ideal plane.

Are these aspirations true of every human soul? The question is a delicate one because the answer must recognize intellectual and moral perversities. It should also note the indifference to those profound values that are real, yet latent, in every psychological structure. What can be asserted here is the fact that in the Christian experiential tradition there is a human constant: the need for conversion to and union with God.

To sum up, first, we should consider all that unites Christians and their different spiritualities. Christ, the Church, the Bible and the liturgy, their condition as children of God, grace: these are the great elements of the common patrimony that unites all souls, whatever may be the special traditions that they profess.

In this connection let us quote some verses from the epistle of St. Paul to the Ephesians in which he explains the profound reasons for Christian unity: "There is one body and one Spirit, even as you were called in one hope of your calling; one Lord, one faith, one baptism; one God and Father of all, who is over all and throughout all, and in us all. But to each one of us grace was given according to the measure of Christ's bestowal" (Eph. 4, 4-7).

All that we have said can characterize Christian spirituality as such, apart from every local or temporal specification. It may even be claimed that what we have written defines the spirituality of the first Christian generations. Yet we should remember that, especially in regard to the "instrumental cause" mentioned above, there has been an evolution, a progressive awareness of the elements of Christian spirituality: hierarchy, sacraments, Scripture, Tradition and liturgy. This awareness was not always expressed in a new spirituality distinct from the spirituality of the beginnings. Christians attained to a better understanding of Christ's message. They also formulated better or different ways of life.

During the apostolic age before revelation was closed, an effort was made to understand Christ's message without any detours or special emphasis either in thinking or acting. Later there was evolution. We find different spiritual climates. Individuals and whole generations of Christians were influenced by personalities, at times powerful, at times gentle. To illustrate this would necessitate an outline of the whole history of Christian spirituality.[6] Rather than do this and wander far afield, let us consider the spiritual climate in which we find ourselves in the 1960s.

The spirituality of the first years of our century was strongly influenced by the teaching of the many schools that rose as the Middle Ages waned and modern times began: the *Devotio moderna,* the Spanish spiritual writers of the 16th century, the French school of the 17th century. Leaders of fifty years ago in some ways distrusted mysticism, a consequence perhaps of the quietism controversies; that they allowed the liturgy to be overshadowed is to be explained as a reaction against the Reformation, and this accounts for the use of formulas of spirituality based on methods of meditation. They were also hesitant about

[6] This was attempted in *Histoire de la spiritualité chrétienne, op. cit.*

the use of the Bible, another form of reaction against the Reformation and all of the individualism, voluntarism and asceticism that it implied.

Since then, however, a change has taken place. New movements have risen in the Church: the liturgical movement, the ecumenical movement and, in the wake of the liturgical movement, the biblical movement. Timeless liturgical and biblical values, suitable to all Christian spiritualities and integral to Christian spirituality as such, were rediscovered. The ecumenical movement brought to light what is good and authentically Christian in the different Christian confessions: for example, in Protestantism, the value of the Bible and of preaching, or in the Eastern Churches, the bond between the mystical life and sacramental life. Furthermore, at the beginning of our century a sharply defined social program became part of Christianity. This was not influenced directly by Marxism, but rather by the rediscovery of apostolic, pastoral, communal and evangelical values which are concretized in the many forms of Catholic Action.

In the 1960s we have reached a situation whereby these different aspirations have succeeded in recovering the privileged charter they enjoyed in the Gospel. This applies to the biblical as well as to the social movement, the ecumenical as well as the liturgical movement. All four movements draw Christians together, no matter how different the formulas of spirituality they may profess, and enable them to rediscover the Gospel and poverty. All agree that Vatican Council II has understood this admirably.

In this area it can be said that Charles de Foucauld takes on the dimensions of a 20th-century prophet: practicing poverty, evangelic and proletarian poverty, living in the midst of men without any particular apostolate except that of being Christ where Christ most needs to be, there, where he is not yet—or is no more.

The present situation should certainly inspire us to be extremely prudent in our judgments and give us at the same time a certain sense of relativity. There is *the* Christian spirituality. It has been defined above. There are Christian spiritualities. But at the present moment we are more and more aware that *a* spirituality has value only insofar as it is rooted in *the* Christian spirituality.

Paul Mikat/*Düsseldorf, Germany*

Collaboration between Clergy and Laity

Any discussion about collaboration between clergy and laity or about the place of the layman in the community must be preceded by theological reflection on the nature of the Church in order to throw some light on the function of the priest and on the vocation and function of the laity.

For a long time the Church has been considered too one-sidedly and exaggeratedly as a juridical corporation or organization which was exclusively represented by the clerical hierarchy. This turned the layman too easily into a mere object of pastoral care. In his essay "On the Unity of the Concept of the Church",[1] Otto Semmelroth has rightly asserted that if we want to see the Church again as essentially the Mystical Body of the Lord, we must reconsider a great number of questions which come to light as soon as we begin to study any aspect of the Church's nature. Among these questions he mentions as typical: the necessity of the Church and Church membership for salvation, the relationship between the spiritual office and the laity, a better definition of the laity within the Church, the nature of the spiritual office and the relation of both its functions to each other. Even a quick glance at these problems will show how compli-

[1] O. Semmelroth, "Um die Einheit des Kirchenbegriffs," in *Fragen der Theologie heute* (Einsiedeln, 1957), pp. 319-35.

61

cated they are. They are certainly not questions that can be solved in a purely juridical and formal way. They are fundamental problems of ecclesiology. They have in common that they can find an answer only in the nature of the Church. They presuppose a specific concept of the Church and any juridical answers can and must take account of previous theological clarifications and conclusions.

We should not overlook here that in the present concern about the concept of the Church we are not merely concerned with *new* views. What Semmelroth said about thinking again of the Church as the Mystical Body of the Lord clearly implies that many ideas appearing in the contemporary ecclesiological debate are drawn from old ecclesiastical literary documents, and especially from patristic literature. The view of the Church as the Mystical Body of Christ has never been wholly forgotten in Catholic theology, but there have been periods when it was pushed into the background. For the historical understanding of the problem it must be constantly emphasized that any treatment of the development of the concept of the Church must take into account the actual controversial situation in the theology of whatever period is under discussion. It is not saying too much that a comprehensive historical presentation of the concept of the Church, if it ever comes to be written, will be at the same time a history of the various controversial situations in the Church.

The Augustinian concept of the Church, for instance, was largely the result of the Donatist controversy and was consequently conditioned by the Donatist insistence on a purely spiritual Church. The decisive changes in the concept of the Church during the later Middle Ages, when the political-minded "publicists" of that period showed little interest in the mystical concept of the Church, cannot be understood without reference to the spiritual development of that time. The one-sided emphasis, in particular, which at that time was put on juridical and institutional problems, must be seen in the light of the great controversies about the conciliar movement. Supporters of the curia fought the conciliarists and both sides were dominated by the canonists. This did not exactly encourage a deeper theological approach to the question of the nature of the Church. In the 16th century, theological controversy on the nature of the Church was obviously conditioned by the extreme spiritualist position taken up by the Reformers.

Theological discussion of the Church in the 20th century has replaced this one-sided picture of the Church by a new approach which corresponds more to the nature of the Church. In his encyclical *Mystici Corporis*[2] Pius XII stated that the Church consists fundamentally of all the faithful and that this teaching must be understood as the original Christian teaching of the Church which the Church has always maintained. The Constitution on the Church[3] says: "Though they differ from one another in essence and not only in degree, the common priesthood of the faithful and the ministerial or hierarchical priesthood are nonetheless interrelated: each of them in its own special way is a participation in the one priesthood of Christ. The ministerial priest, by the sacred power he enjoys, teaches and rules the priestly people; acting in the person of Christ, he performs the eucharistic sacrifice, and offers it to God in the name of all the people. But the faithful, in virtue of their royal priesthood, join in the offering of the eucharist. They likewise exercise that priesthood in receiving the sacraments, in prayer and thanksgiving, in the witness of a holy life, and by self-denial and active charity." [4] The fact that the laity, too, have an active part in the "royal priesthood" shows that it is a constitutive element of the unity of all the faithful, whether ordained or not, and shows their collaboration as a common interaction of the various members of one body.

Etymologically the laity are those who constitute the People (*laos*) of God. They are the "chosen race", the "holy people". If there is nevertheless a basic distinction between the clergy and

[2] Pius XII, Encyclical *Mystici Corporis,* of June 29, 1943, in *Acta Apostolicae Sedis* 35 (1943), p. 208.
[3] *The Constitution on the Church* (Glen Rock, N.J.: Paulist Press, 1965).
[4] *Ibid.,* Art. 10.

the laity, it follows that the laity is the "normal" condition of the Christian faithful. Priests and monks are exceptions, not because they have been promised a better existence, but because they have been selected within the Church for the sake of a *special* service to the faithful: "For the distinction that the Lord made between sacred ministers and the rest of the People of God bears within it a certain union, since pastors and the other faithful are bound to each other by a mutual necessity. Pastors of the Church, following the example of the Lord, should minister to one another and to the other faithful. These in their turn should enthusiastically lend their joint assistance to their pastors and teachers. Thus in their diversity all bear witness to the wonderful unity in the body of Christ. This very diversity of graces, ministries and works gathers the children of God into one, because 'all these things are the work of one and the same spirit' (1 Cor. 12, 11)." [5]

It would therefore be a distortion of the Church's design if collaboration between clergy and laity were taken to mean that the two positions were interchangeable, and one could take the place of the other. This would do justice to neither priest nor layman. The priest is, by his ordination, directed to a definite and carefully limited field of activity within the Church: he conveys the Word and the sacrament. "Among the principal duties of bishops the preaching of the Gospel occupies an eminent place." [6] Ordination bestows on him a "character" (sign) which cannot be lost. But this implies that he is given a field of activity which excludes him from other functions which belong specifically to the laity. "What specifically characterizes the laity is their secular nature. It is true that those in holy orders can at times be engaged in secular activities, and even have a secular profession. But they are, by reason of their particular vocation, especially and professedly ordained to the sacred ministry. Similarly, by their state in life, religious give splendid and striking testimony that the world cannot be transformed and offered to

[5] *Ibid.*, Art. 32.
[6] *Ibid.*, Art. 25.

God without the spirit of the beatitudes. But the laity, by their special vocation, seek the kingdom of God by engaging in temporal affairs and by ordering them according to the plan of God. They live in the world, that is, in each and in all of the secular professions and occupations. They live in the ordinary circumstances of family and social life, from which the very web of their existence is woven. Today they are called by God that by exercising their proper function, and led by the spirit of the Gospel, they may work for the sanctification of the world from within as a leaven. In this way they may make Christ known to others, especially by the testimony of a life resplendent in faith, hope and charity." [7]

There is no legitimate "flight from the world" for the laity. If they withdrew from the world and from work within the world they would leave the field open for occupation by unbelief. "Moreover, let the laity also by their combined efforts remedy the customs and conditions of the world, if they are an inducement to sin, so that they all may be conformed to the norms of justice and may favour the practice of virtue rather than hinder it. By so doing they will imbue culture and human activity with genuine moral values." [8] Lay piety consists essentially in that the layman does justice to the tasks which his place in the world assigns to him and sees this activity as a religious function and obligation. Speaking of this function of the laity the Constitution says: "Therefore, since they are tightly bound up in all types of temporal affairs, it is their special task to order and to throw light upon these affairs in such a way that they may be made and grow according to Christ to the praise of the creator and redeemer." [9] This can mean only that the layman's way to Christ lies objectively and precisely in the *proper discharge* of this function. The question, then, whether a layman should be ordained deacon is therefore far from being the most important in our discussion (since in any case he would basically cease to be "lay" in the full

[7] *Ibid.*, Art. 31.
[8] *Ibid.*, Art. 36.
[9] *Ibid.*, Art. 31.

sense of the word if he is ordained). Nor is it a question of whether more lay people should be trained as catechists. The primary issue is the laity's responsibility for the world.

What, however, does this mean in practice? It means that for the layman who lives in Christ and is as such fully aware of his existence in the Church, nothing can remain indifferent in this world, in his piece of the world, in the sector of the cosmos where he has to fulfill his function. If he looked on the "piece of world" for which he is specifically responsible as "religiously meaningless" and "indifferent", there would be a loss of responsibility for, and control of, the world. He would then cease to be religious himself in the true sense of the word.

In this connection the Constitution refers especially to the profound meaning of marriage and family: "In this undertaking great importance clearly attaches to that state of life that is sanctified by a special sacrament, namely, married and family life. For where Christianity pervades the entire mode of family life, and increasingly transforms it, one will find there both the practice and an excellent school of the lay apostolate. In such a home husbands and wives find their proper vocation in being witnesses of the faith and love of Christ to one another and to their children. The Christian family loudly proclaims both the present virtues of the kingdom of God and the hope of a blessed life to come. Thus, by its example and its witness it accuses the world of sin and enlightens those who seek the truth." [10]

The priest, too, is aware of this responsibility for the world; for him, too, the world constitutes a task to fulfill, but not in the same immediate way as for the layman. The priest must proclaim the word of the Lord in a special way. Because of the authenticity of his spiritual word, the Church dispenses him by and large from proclaiming the unspiritual word which can never be as urgent and sacrosanct as the spiritual word. Yet, this priestly task must be fulfilled in collaboration with the community. Collaboration, therefore, between clergy and laity means above all

[10] *Ibid.*, Art. 35.

communing in the celebration of the sacred functions, the celebration of Mass. Gerald Philips rightly points out in his book on the *Role of the Laity in the Church*[11] that the sacrificial formula of the liturgy is in the plural: *"per quem tibi offerimus"* (through whom we offer to you).

Participation in the Mass and in prayer is therefore never achieved by a merely passive presence. Nor should it be misunderstood as a purely subjective concern, by which the worshipper somehow leaves the community behind and gives himself to a purely individualistic experience of his faith, independent of the community. "We are a community at prayer, not a gathering of individuals who look for help," says Philips. "Christ, our Mediator, the principal Actor and Leader of the liturgy, offers his Father adoration, request and thanksgiving with a single voice, and he obtains a favourable hearing for us through his union with the Church. The one Spirit unites us in the unity of merciful love." Only when we see the liturgy in this light does the liturgical movement have any theological meaning. It is not a matter of changes in ceremonies, but of understanding what the liturgy is and always must be by its very nature.

It is therefore not doing justice to our Catholic faith when we seek the primary place for this collaboration between clergy and laity elsewhere than in the sacramental context of the Church. Here the community is united with Christ, here is the sacrament, here the promise, which justifies the name of "People of God", of *laos theou,* for the assembled community. Every other kind of collaboration between clergy and laity is based on this one. That is why it is necessary to distinguish carefully between the functions of the priest and those of the laity. This makes sure that the collaboration is rightly understood. "The lay apostolate, however, is a participation in the salvific mission of the Church itself. Through their baptism and confirmation all are commissioned to that apostolate by the Lord himself. Moreover, by the

[11] G. Philips, *De Leek in de Kerk* (Louvain, 1951). English trans.: *Role of the Laity in the Church* (Montreal-Paris, 1955).

sacraments, especially the holy eucharist, that charity toward God and man which is the soul of all apostolate is communicated and nourished." [12]

The Church, however, is in the world and turned toward the world. Priests and laity share the apostolic mission to take the Gospel into the world. I said that this mission applies in a special sense to the layman insofar as he has a definite place in the world. But he does not stand alone here. The communion of the Church, the promise and fulfillment which he has experienced at the Mass, make him, as he is now in the world, refer again to the Church and to the priest in his special function within the Church. In practice this means that, although the layman has an apostolic mission which he discharges on his own responsibility, it is precisely this apostolic character which makes him turn again to the Church and the priest as the minister of the sacraments.

The communion of priests and laity in the community does not allow of any autonomy on either side. It is rather like this: the layman refers back to the priest in his worldly mission, while the priest cannot do without the example of a Christian way of life as offered by the laity, understood in the right sense. "For all their works, prayers and apostolic endeavors, their ordinary married and family life, their daily occupations, their physical and mental relaxation, if carried out in the Spirit, and even the hardships of life, if patiently borne—all become 'spiritual sacrifices acceptable to God through Jesus Christ' (1 Peter 2, 5)".[13]

The priest has to rely on the vitality of the faith in the community, otherwise he will become isolated: "Let pastors recognize and promote the dignity as well as the responsibility of the laity in the Church. Let them willingly employ their prudent advice. Let them confidently assign duties to them in the service of the Church, allowing them freedom and room for action. Further, let pastors encourage lay people so that they may undertake tasks on their own initiative. Attentively in Christ, let them

[12] *Constitution, op. cit.,* Art. 33.
[13] *Ibid.,* Art. 34.

consider with fatherly love the projects, suggestions and desires proposed by the laity." [14]

Here is perhaps the place to mention the importance of that mutual discussion, advice and general assistance in life which are so vital for a community. This is not only a matter of the priest giving advice to the layman, but also of the priest being given advice by the laity because, bearing a special responsibility for the souls of the community, the priest would fail in his task if he ignored consultation and dialogue with the members of his community. The effective guidance given by the priest depends in actual fact on what the priest knows about the problems and difficulties of our time. The solutions he has to offer cannot be deduced from particular theological truths, but presuppose a practical knowledge and experience of the most varied kind. Here the priest has to rely on the laity. In many fields of human experience the layman is to a great extent more knowledgeable. Only when he brings this to the priest in the spirit of collaboration can pastoral work be successful.

From this point of view one might well revise the place and function of a great number of Catholic societies in the Church. The great lay organizations have to make sure that there is room in the world for Catholic life. The center of this is the liturgical service. The center of the organizations is the priest. The field in which the organizations exercise their activity is the world. The collaboration between the clergy and the lay organizations is therefore subject to the same criteria as that between the priest and the individual layman. It accords with the mission to proclaim the Kingdom of God on this earth, or, as St. Peter says, to become "a holy priesthood, to offer spiritual sacrifices acceptable to God through Jesus Christ" (1 Peter 2, 5).

These various functions can, of course, overlap, but one should look at this in a positive way. Just as the lay organization should do its work in an independent and adult fashion without losing its relation with the priest, so it is possible for the laity to take

[14] *Ibid.,* Art. 37.

over certain tasks, particularly in the *diakonia,* the "service", by taking part in the assistance given to the needy members of the community. This kind of work is often and too easily left to the priest. The same holds for teaching. To mark the exact boundary in this field in a casuistic manner would not only be misguided but, by the nature of the case, wrong. "Besides this apostolate, which certainly pertains to all Christians, the laity can also be called in various ways to a more direct form of cooperation in the apostolate of the hierarchy. This was the way certain men and women assisted Paul the apostle in the Gospel, labouring much in the Lord (cf. Phil. 4, 3; Rom. 16, 3ff.). Further, they have the capacity to assume from the hierarchy certain ecclesiastical functions that are to be performed for a spiritual purpose." [15]

However important this use of collaboration may be in particular instances, and however symptomatic this official doctrine may be of the development which is taking place within the Church, it remains nevertheless only a part of the collaboration that is possible between clergy and laity, and by no means the most important part. This collaboration presupposes essentially that both sides respect each other's proper position and, with this respect for each other's independence, find means of cooperation. To misunderstand the proper character of each other's function and of mutual relationship would be dangerous for both the priest and the layman. But mutual respect would bring out the meaning of the fact that both are members of the one Church which they serve and whose head is Christ.

[15] *Ibid.,* Art. 33.

Edouard Ranwez/*Namur, Belgium*

The Three
Evangelical Counsels

The conciliar Constitution on the Church (Chapters V and VI) declared that the call to sanctity was universal and paid homage to the irreplaceable service to the Church rendered by the religious institutes. In doing so it focused the attention of the faithful on the ideal they have in common and on the particular means for attaining it. Current belief maintains that "the best means" for sanctification lie in the effective and integral practice of the "counsels" commonly designated as "evangelical".

This manner of speaking (not altogether recent) may be quite legitimate if the terms in quotation marks are properly defined and understood in a wholly relative sense. These terms must nevertheless be used with caution when given an absolute bearing. Since Vatican Council II has stirred up new interest in these problems they well deserve some thought. We may begin then, with a question.

(a) When we speak of these matters in an absolute sense, can we be reasonably certain that all forms of renunciation implied in the practice of the "evangelical counsels" are "the best means" of attaining perfection? If man's condition had not been deteriorated by original sin, should he not consider the normal use of sex, among other things, as an integral part of highly desirable human conduct instead of regarding it as a moral danger? In the

71

present state of a nature that is fallen and has been regained by Christ, perfect chastity undoubtedly constitutes, for those whose personal vocation makes them capable of it, the best means of escaping from the tyranny of carnal desires and thereby progressing toward perfection with greater freedom. But it seems to me that this undoubted excellence of the "evangelical counsel" regarding the use of the senses is wholly relative both in respect to mankind at large and to any particular individual. The state of virginity "in itself" (*i.e.,* in the abstract, though taking account of the present situation) is said to be more perfect than that of married life. Nevertheless, those called to the state of marriage find this state to be of higher value than the virginity of the celibate, particularly when they reflect on the sacramental grace meant to transpose this mutual love into an exquisite charity that becomes constantly more operative.

(b) Just as the phrase "best means" cannot be taken absolutely, neither can the phrase "evangelical counsel" be used without certain precisions if it is to be understood in the exact sense. This is true of many formulas in common use: they are congenitally loaded with ambiguities. In order not to fall victim to them, they should be carefully analyzed. Let us therefore concentrate on removing the ambiguity connected with the classical formula: the "three evangelical counsels", accomplishing this by careful consideration of three questions that bear on the three words that make up this formula:

1. Are there really only three "evangelical counsels"?
2. In what sense are these evangelical instructions "counsels"?
3. In what sense are these "counsels" "evangelical"?

1. Are the "Evangelical Counsels" Limited to Three in Number?

If we commonly speak of the three evangelical counsels the reason seems to be that the virtues they recommend commonly constitute for us the matter of the three public vows of religion.

In reality, the Gospel contains far more recommendations

than these three. Apart from the two virtues,[1] humility and gentleness, which our Lord recommended to us for imitation in a particularly formal manner when he said, "Learn from me that I am gentle and humble of heart", all kinds of more or less radical forms of renouncement should be noted. They are demanded of anyone who wants to follow the Master and have part in his kingdom; the entire life of the Lord on this earth constitutes a perfect example of such renouncements. Of all the various explicit or implicit exhortations to follow Christ's example, one can certainly say that they also are "evangelical counsels". Nevertheless, it must be pointed out that the idea of counsel, in the strict sense of the word, is only clearly expressed twice in the Gospel: first, when the Lord declared that spiritual castration is only suitable for those "who can understand", and second, when he suggested to the young rich man that he should give away his worldly goods in order to play his personal part in the economy of salvation. On this basis, therefore, there would be only two evangelical counsels in the strict sense of the word.

It does not seem likely that one could obtain the number of three by examining the primitive apostolic tradition which might reflect the teaching of the Gospel more adequately on this point. There were undoubtedly from the beginning of the apostolic era some fervent Christians who concentrated on the ascetic practice of one or another virtue recommended by Christ. There were virgins, pious widows, the voluntary poor who, individually or in groups, practiced the teaching of the Master and his representatives with particular care. However, this does not indicate that the first Christians held convictions which can be expressed in terms comparable to those later prevalent among religious who were trained to a strictly organized cenobitical existence. Only historians can decide at what precise time this trio of "evan-

[1] *Two* virtues or *one* only, depending upon whether one considers the double aspect of the same basic attitude of the world toward either God (humility) or one's fellowmen (gentleness), or whether one considers the many-sided aspect of their one common root (charity that renders the soul true and ready for service).

gelical counsels" became part of current terminology. But it seems certain that the virtues officially practiced in religious houses were customarily labelled as "the three counsels" only at a much later date.

Moreover, if we want to equate the number of evangelical counsels to that of public religious vows, we should also take into account the supplementary vows pronounced by some religious institutes. This would bring the number of evangelical counsels well beyond the three consecrated by custom.

In any event, why should we want to identify certain practices *counselled* in the Gospel with practices *vowed* at a religious-profession ceremony? One can bind oneself by vow to anything that is honest, whether or not it is already the object of a precept. In this case the vow would simply have the effect of strengthening an obligation already contained in the precept. On the other hand, nothing prevents us from binding ourselves to a purely optional line of conduct without binding ourselves by a vow. And so, the conciliar fathers pointed out (n. 39) that the practice of what are called the evangelical counsels can be observed not only in a condition or state officially sanctioned by the Church but also on a private basis (which presupposes entire freedom on this point). We should add that in the Oriental Church the vow is not linked up with monastic life as it is in the West, and that even in the West canon law recognizes secular institutes and societies without vows.

Finally, it should be noted that although the Gospel recommends certain practices which, in fact, have become the object of religious vows, it nowhere mentions these vows as such.

In short, it is an illusion to think and speak as though a necessary and exclusive relation existed between the idea of an evangelical counsel and the way of life reserved to religious profession.

2. *Are the Evangelical Counsels in Question Only*
   "Counsels" in the Strict Sense of the Word?

The answer to this question is both affirmative and negative. They are simply "counsels" in the sense that they are not general precepts. They are not simply counsels and "nothing but counsels" if this would mean that these evangelical counsels, recommended in general to everybody, would never constitute for anyone the *occasion* or *object* of a veritable obligation in conscience. Precepts govern, in an imperative and uniform way, all to whom they are directed. To violate a precept or a law is, objectively speaking, always wrong; no one is ever permitted to blaspheme or to slander. On the other hand, failure to follow a counsel is not necessarily wrong. It might, on the contrary, be a very good thing. As Thomas Aquinas says, a counsel is essentially optional and is therefore left to each one's discretion. If, in all sincerity, I deem that a particular counsel does not correspond to what God expects of me here and now, I am not bound to follow it; but if I think that such a counsel suits my personal vocation to great advantage, I am positively in error if I do not follow it.

This does not change the counsel itself into a command; it simply indicates that, on occasion, one may be bound by natural law or Christian charity to follow a good counsel, just as one may find oneself bound to accept a wholly free invitation or not to ignore a sensible suggestion. It often happens that actions which, objectively speaking, are "morally indifferent" nevertheless are *commanded* by circumstances. Why then should actions that are generally advisable because "better in themselves" (*e.g.,* almsgiving) not be *demanded* on occasion because of a properly understood self-interest, or the love of neighbor or of God?

In fact, nowhere in the Gospel is there mention of two kinds of norms, of which one kind (the precepts) would always be obligatory and the other kind (the counsels) never required.[2]

In Matthew 22, 40 Christ recalls the great commandment of Deuteronomy 6, 5 (the first) and of Leviticus 19, 18 (the second), and he completes this basic precept by what he calls in

[2] No serious objection can be alleged by referring to Matthew 19, 16-23. This passage does not deal with a general norm but with one particular case which is literally unique; it does not refer to moral liberty but to psychological liberty, as is indicated by the words: "If you wish . . . to enter into life", of verse 17 of the same chapter. Equally erroneous would be an objection based on the grammatical form of St. Paul, 1 Cor. 7, 28-38.

John 13, 34 *his new* commandment: ". . . as I have loved you".

On the basis of this authentic charter, everyone is bound to do *all he can* for the greater glory of God and the good of all. Within the framework of this general law there is room for the greatest diversity in the ways we plan our life, but all these ways must by all means be inspired by the same maximal charity according to each one's capacity. All must love "with all their strength"; but this strength differs from one person to another. Each one, therefore, must see for himself how he can fulfill the common obligation of giving himself, body and soul, to the service of his Lord and his brothers.

All must obviously respect the great prohibitions contained in natural law. In general, positive law, too, will lay down the same obligation for all those subject to it (unless they are excused because of some physical or moral impossibility). Lastly, we should retain the category, rather imprecise, of "duties of state" which, roughly speaking, covers the obligations inherent in a given profession or social condition.

But beyond these indications, which are approximately valid for each class of individuals, one must also take account of the numberless obligations that are more or less clearly contained in them and which, commanded by often unforeseeable circumstances, apply to each particular individual according to his individual disposition and his wholly personal vocation.

At the bottom of these "individualized" duties of state there are only motives and ways of behavior which are strictly unique in this world since from the moral point of view no one's situation can be completely identical to that of his neighbor. It is therefore of little importance whether the immediate norm of the action we take is a precept or a counsel. The essential point is that we act, in all good faith, according to a rule, immediate or distant, to which all our choices are subject if we wish to act rationally.

It makes no difference whether we obey a formal commandment of Christ (My commandment is that you love one another . . .), or whether we put into practice a less imperative-looking injunction (Learn from me that I am humble . . .), if, ultimately, we find ourselves compelled by love to follow the example of the Master.

Ultimately, therefore, we may easily place under the heading of "evangelical counsels" anything that is not clearly the equivalent of a commandment which applies without distinction to every way of life. We are tempted to call it a counsel because it is not clearly and equally derived from the supreme commandment which virtually contains all the others. This applies as soon as we leave the level of minimal renouncement which is demanded of all without exception.

Thus, for example, all owe obedience—and perfect obedience —to those who represent God's authority; but not all should opt for what is called "religious obedience". All must be poor in spirit and even, up to a certain point, practice effectively that poverty that dispenses with superfluities, but obviously not all should dispose of all their goods. All must observe a relative chastity, according to their state of life, but, again, not all should profess perfect and perpetual chastity. But I wish to repeat that all these different forms of virtue not prescribed in a universal manner may nevertheless, on occasion, impose themselves upon those who without question would recognize in such practices a personal invitation from the Lord. To love God "with all one's heart" excludes any deliberate and conscious determination to displease him.

In conclusion, the three "evangelical counsels" are optional, because not universally imposed, but on occasion a privileged conscience may find itself compelled to pursue the object of these counsels.

3. In What Sense Can These Three "Counsels" Be Called "Evangelical"?

The answer to this question will be brief since it is implied in the two preceding answers.

There is no doubt that the primary elements that led to the creation of religious institutes in the Church are found in the

Gospel. The inspiration contained in Christ's teaching and example has gradually led to the organization of what is conventionally called "religious life".

For that matter, anything that constitutes moral perfection and contributes to its fulfillment finds in Christ its living example. It is he who emphasized (Mark 10, 24) how difficult it is for the rich to attain to the kingdom of God. It is he who praised (Matt. 19, 12) the renunciation of the virgins. It is he who provided the example of perfect obedience by his total submission to the will of the Father, and who declared (John 4, 34) that this obedience (his nourishment) was the essence of his mission on this earth and, as such, was the condition of any redemptive mission. Therefore, those who, for the love of Christ, definitely and publicly renounce their worldly goods, the satisfaction of the flesh and their independence, can rightly claim that they base their conduct on the Gospel and are entitled to call the rules they observe for love of the Savior "evangelical".

But this does not mean that the actual structure of religious life and the public profession that constitutes its initiation are "divinely instituted" or of a direct evangelical origin. This depends directly on the Church. Everything that has contributed to the development of monastic rules and to the slow evolution that led from sporadic anchoretic or cenobitical attempts at religious life to the definitive organization of orders and congregations as we know them—all this is due to a thousand contingent factors intimately linked with the history of the Church over a number of centuries. It was only very gradually that the deepest aspirations of virtuous men and women toward the contemplative or apostolic ideal took shape in official formulas, incorporated in canon law.

It is therefore only at a relatively late date that one could apply the terminology in use today, a use which at first implied and then lost sight of the necessary distinctions detailed in this article. It was only in the long run that it became accepted custom to see in the threefold formula of "obedience, poverty and chastity" the equivalent of the appropriate means of ensuring a certain and rapid rise to perfection, to the point of describing these means without further qualification as the "evangelical counsels", as if they alone represented the program for sanctity in an authentic fashion. In other words, although it is right to say that the three great vows of religion correspond to *some* evangelical counsels, it would be wrong to think that *the* evangelical counsels are exclusively the subject of religious profession in religious institutes.

All that has been said here is, I think, in agreement with the teaching of the Council in Chapters V and VI of the Constitution on the Church. The proof can be found in those first two phrases of the chapter dealing with the religious (Art. 43). The first begins like this: "The evangelical counsels . . . are based on the words and example of the Lord." [3] And the second: "Church authority has taken care, under the inspiration of the Holy Spirit, to interpret these evangelical counsels, to regulate their practice and finally to build on them stable forms of living." [4]

[3] In his use of this passage of the Magna Carta, G. Dejaifve translates "The public profession of the evangelical counsels, based on . . ." where the conciliar text says "The evangelical counsels, based on . . ." (*Nouv. Rev. Théol.*, Jan., 1965, p. 19). This discrepancy seems to reinforce the ambiguity I am trying to eliminate.

[4] *Constitution on the Church* (Glen Rock, N.J.: Paulist Press, 1965), p. 155.

Etienne Cornélis, O.P./*Nijmegen, Netherlands*

Christian Spirituality and Non-Christian Spiritualities

The first flowering of "comparative mystical theology" kept pace with the Modernist crisis. As a result it remained suspect in the eyes of the champions of orthodoxy in Protestant as well as in Roman Catholic camps. Many "liberals", however, welcomed it with an enthusiasm which at times was to rush them along the path of unfounded fancies common to theosophy through the ages.

It is an undeniable fact that many striking parallels are possible among the mystical phenomena of the various "metaphysical" traditions of both East and West (cf. the traditionalist doctrine of René Guénon). These are explained in part by the common origins of the most representative branches of the great traditions of mysticism. Moreover, what cannot be explained by historical affinities can at times be explained by what have been labeled "anthropisms", that is, the set of characteristics (*jeu de caractères*) common to all men in all times and in all places.

In regard to the first point, the study of the origins of Hellenistic and ancient Indian mysticism has led many reliable experts to recognize a probable common origin in a certain type of Shamanism (Dodd, M. Eliade). The archaic forms of this Shamanism would be relatively well preserved—thus constituting a type of "living fossil"—in the cultural traditions of Northern

81

and Central Asia. From this common source would have issued in the East the form of asceticism which we know as Yoga. Moving toward the West, it would have given rise to the Orphic-Pythagorean movement which was to branch out and expand into neo-Pythagorism, Gnosticism, neo-Platonism and the mysticism of Eastern Christianity.

In both the East and the West one finds on the one hand a certain metaphysico-religious problematic embodied in a dialectical opposition between monism and dualism. Closely related to this problematic on the other hand is the transmission of practical "experimental" procedures, a kind of psychosomatic *"haute école"* which aims at bringing about states of consciousness "free" from the ordinary contingencies of sense knowledge. However, the fact that these are closely related could be explained without recourse to historical connections. We could as a matter of fact view this as an "anthropism", that is, the inevitable corollary resulting from a speculative reflection that takes as its starting point some "unitive" experience.

A better historical and phenomenological knowledge of the manifestations of Eastern mysticism as well as a deepening of Western philosophical anthropology along existential lines did indeed give hope of a more exact classification of the different types of mysticism. But the essential point of view of the method remains in fact intimately bound up with both the evolution of the post-Kantian problematic and its repercussions on the problem of faith and revelation.

In this perspective, the great importance which apologists of spiritualism attach to the study of mystical phenomena is easily explained. We are living at a time when the word "metaphysical", embraced by the apostles of an ambiguous theosophy, takes on the chimerical meaning of anything that escapes empirical verification. The question of comparing spiritualities then draws its importance from the most burning philosophical issue of our day: "experience and metaphysics".

The study of the converging factors among mystical phenomena has led several Catholic authors (O. Lacombe, L. Gardet), in the wake of the Thomism of Maritain, to reopen the question posed by the first students of comparative mysticism. They have tried to account for the manifest similarities, being careful at the same time to avoid the mistakes and confusion of those who preceded them.

On the other hand, many Protestant theologians, unable to discover reliable criteria for distinguishing "natural" and "supernatural" mysticism, and disturbed at seeing Modernism gain a foothold in "natural theology", will tread the path, urged by Barth and his followers, that leads to a radical refusal of all forms of spiritual method, Christian as well as non-Christian. The very notion of a spiritual itinerary seems to them to imply some sort of necessary continuity—and consequently one blasphemous to the God of the Bible—between end and means, between the creator and the creature he has drawn from nothingness.

It is against this polemical background that we can best view the intentions, secret or avowed, of the majority of Western authors who write about Eastern spirituality. An apologetic preoccupation tends in general to vitiate their efforts at understanding. Despite all the ardor they bring to the debate, the problem which motivated their interest remains unsolved. By way of compensation, the great number of works that have been written on the subject have placed us in a better position to know the facts. As a result we will be forced to reinterpret our information and change some of our judgments which at first were somewhat too clear-cut in that they were made a priori (R. Otto, *Mystique d'Orient et mystique d'Occident*).

A convenient way for the theologian to disentangle himself from the thorny problem posed by mystical phenomena is to consider them as a result of a psychosomatic technique which would have empirically gained control of certain structures of the nervous system. Such a concept has a large measure of truth, in many cases, as has been shown by the combined use of the electro-cardiograph and the electro-encephalograph on Indian yogis in a state of *samâdhi*.

Therefore, from the point of view of moral theology, the use
of these techniques concerned the theologian only indirectly,
just as eroticism—to which a Freudian-inspired anthropology
would also reduce mystical phenomena—became the domain
of classical theology only insofar as it provided matter for a
moral judgment in the light of revelation. However, it must be
noted that, if certain types of mysticism fit neatly into this sketch,
there are others that do not, beginning with the most authentic
forms of Buddhist asceticism and mysticism.

One fact in particular cannot escape the attention of the
theologian. Many of the paths proposed by mysticism, particularly that of the East, advocate one or another form of impermanence (*dépassement*) of the empirical world and its laws even
to the point of urging disciples to scorn or flee from moral
commitments. It would even seem that this is precisely that
"beyond good and evil" which captivates certain initiates who
are ever ready to submit to the rigors of long ascetical prepara-
tions for states of ecstacy or trance. At times these exercises are
rigorously calculated with the purpose of attaining a state of
quietism which paralyzes the moral conscience.

As we suggested above, the tenets of Oriental philosophical
monism could well be only the thematization, in rational terms,
of experiences of this type. Nevertheless, due to the ambiguous
nature of apophatic expressions, it remains equally possible to
conceive of them as being in an entirely different genre of experience. In some cases, reasonably reliable indications lead us
to believe that the purpose of the mystic philosopher is precisely
to safeguard the orientation of thought against every relapse
into an immanentist conception of the absolute (Shankara).
In other respects, it is almost the rule in the East that on his
journey the mystic must pass through a stage of profound moral
purification. The question, then, is to discover whether this
preparation plays a purely propaedeutic role, or whether there
is a continuity in meaning between it and the mystical experience
for which it prepares. While insisting very much on the indispensable methodical effort of the ascetic, many masters of East-

ern spirituality nevertheless describe the irruption of this supreme experience as a grace, a gratuitous gift.

This has hampered the search for a reliable criterion by which we may distinguish natural and supernatural mysticism. Can we even set up a parallel between "natural experience" and "supernatural experience"? Or, are we not forced to recognize that the terms "experience" and "supernatural" are already mutually exclusive? The latter perspective in judging mystical phenomena is closely allied to that of R. Bultmann and those who follow him in insisting on the demythologization of statements about the supernatural. The Christian mystique of baptism, which "assimilates" the neophyte to Christ in his death and resurrection, appears in the judgment of this school (which is inspired by the works of the *Religionsgeschichtliche Schule*) as one example among others of a mystico-mythical structure. This is also found in the initiation rites (*expérience initiatique*) of the Shaman (medicine man) just as in the "sacramental" participation by the faithful in the lot of their god-savior in mystery religions.

Again, the dismissal by certain theologians of some Eastern forms of mysticism is based on considerations of another order, related to, but not identical with, those arising from an "immanence-transcendence" dialectic. Stressing the primacy of charity (*agapé*) and the spirituality of the Sermon on the Mount as the special characteristics of Christianity, they dismiss as foreign to its spirit any spirituality that does not have at its center moral commitment in inter-personal relationships. Orthodox Calvinism, in its attempt to get to the bottom of the "advantage" of Christianity, divorces faith from every type of mysticism in the name of the opposition between *eros* and *agapé* (Nygren). It is, as a matter of fact, relatively easy to distinguish the phenomena inspired by evangelical Christianity from those which appear in the line of a monist tradition of either neo-Platonic or Vedantine inspiration.

Within these mysticizing currents (*courants mysticisants*), the *noûs* and the *âtman* are to be restored to their essential purity at the point where they meet with the One or with Saccidananda, the ineffable ground of all being and of all beatitude. Discernment, nevertheless, is no longer easy when it comes to forms of spirituality based on the ardent, loving search for an embrace with the Absolute who comes to meet his lovers under the perceptible form of an Avatar (krishnaism) and who, for the sake of the primacy of love, refuses in a state of consciousness a union without distinction as proposed by monist schools. Often we are obliged to note a remarkable kinship of ideas and of sentiments between these forms of "erotic" mysticism (the Indian *bhaktiyoga*) and those developed in the Christian West along traditional lines. At the threshold of the latter is found Origen's Commentary on the Canticle of Canticles. One difference, however, remains clearly visible: only rarely do the Eastern mystiques of love stress as forcefully as their Christian parallels the indivisible unity of justice and love.

Most of the great religious spiritualities culminate in a mystical experience of an ineffable nature. This does not mean necessarily that they are simply interchangeable. Each must be studied in its proper religious and cultural context. This context is important for the internal structure of an experience that cannot be translated into concepts, a structure that has a definite place in the prolongation of a line supported by this or that mythical prop of the imagination. All who specialize in the mystical teaching of John of the Cross have stressed the intimate connection between the experience that it supposes and the diction of the images chosen by the mystical poet. Nor is it immaterial either that the highest type of experience results from this rather than that ascetical practice, for the nature of the preparation very probably determines the quality of the experience in which it culminates.

Conversely, every school of spirituality gives particular attention to the "means" which it judges to be in harmony with the type of supreme experience it envisions. On this level, a dialogue between spiritualities becomes possible and very probably desirable and promising. The sort of benefit that we can hope for from such a dialogue has been very aptly labeled "cross-fertilization" (W. King). "Archetypal images" have a very serviceable and necessary role when a man begins to follow the path that should lead to the mastery of his passions, to the liberation from the exercise of his higher faculties through detachment from all ego-centered thought and will activity, in a word, to the integral "adultization" of the man. In this sense, mysticism and "paideia" coincide, as Philo of Alexandria was one of the first to realize.

In this order of ideas, if we admit that each culture has not only its own familial demons but its tutelary angels as well, the man who wishes to fulfill himself integrally, to reconstitute his interior "pleroma"—according to the myth-image once used in the Church as well as among Gnostics—such a man will have to become universal in order to be able to make use of all the tongues of myth without becoming dominated by any of them. The doctrine of Philo the Jew, situated at the crossroads of a mysticizing Hellenism and a pythagorizing Judaism, prefigures Christian spirituality in that it proposes a spiritual itinerary that "destroys" nothing legitimate but "accomplishes" all, without at the same time falling into syncretism of undifferentiated mysticism. It owes its singular force to the fact that it preserves the premises of a monotheistic theory of creation, its inheritance from Israel.

On the other hand, Gnosticism, heir of the majority of Philo's theses, did fall away from the straight line of tradition in believing that it was discovering in "ecstatic" gnosis the impermanence (*dépassement*) and annihilation of a faith that was reduced to a propaedeutic stage without continuity with the final goal. Together with Origen, the Gnostic theme of the "ascent" through the spheres of the "powers" has found a rightful place in the doctrine of the Church. Here, it is faith which alone constitutes the moving force capable of a *dépassement;* this same faith, which empties ascetico-mystical "perfections" of their "pretentiousness", is alone in a position to achieve, in humble submission, the definitive emancipation of those who, by means of it, transcend and at the same time fulfill the order of "justice" and of "law" which is the order of the "powers" that govern this world.

By way of a brief conclusion to this rapid survey of the issues involved, we pause for a moment to consider, from a Christian point of view, the dangers we have to fear, as well as the benefits we can hope for, as a result of an exchange of ideas between Christian and non-Christian spiritualities. The danger of considering all religious traditions as equally valid insofar as all, supposedly, converge finally toward the same mystical summit (making relative everything of a confessional nature in them) is certainly not illusory. It seems, nevertheless, that the Roman Catholic and the Eastern Christian are more immune to this syncretist disorder than the faithful of some Protestant sects. These latter, for cultural as well as religious reasons, are very eager to free themselves from the narrow confines of a certain "fundamentalism". Proneness on the part of Protestants to succumb to forms of mysticism manifests itself particularly toward Indian mysticism in English-speaking countries, either in places where it was introduced by the English who had lived in India or by Indians educated in England (Aurobindo, Radhakrishnan). As a matter of fact, it is the present President of the Republic of India that the Dutch Calvinist apologist, H. Kraemer, has chosen as his scapegoat in a book in which he opposes Christian "faith" and non-Christian "religions".

We shall not go further than those modern representatives of the spirit of Gnosticism who seek to reconcile, and at the same time to make relative, all the individual religious traditions for the sake of a "metaphysical" mysticism. A movement is taking shape, akin spiritually to that which aims at demythologizing statements about the supernatural, which W. King has admirably defined: "Will such a change unrecognizably dilute and weaken the strong sense of divine-human fellowship and communion that has been the fountain-head of Christian devotion in the past into a theosophical-mystical type of impersonal awareness and contemplation?"[1] Without wishing to minimize the danger of the slow erosion of Christian personalism, it nevertheless seems to us that the advantages we can look forward to from close contact with non-Christian mysticisms are of very great importance, at least for those Christians whose faith has not remained infantile.

We limit ourselves to two examples which seem to us to strike with precision the two levels on which this meeting of spiritualities effects the cross-fertilization mentioned above. The first is of a missionary in India, an excellent and knowledgeable judge of Indian spirituality, Fr. Neuner. Apropos of the attempt of Fr. Deschanet to adapt in the East the methods of Hatha-Yoga to the spiritual framework of the Christian ascetic, he writes: "This endeavor is based on the correct hypothesis that an authentically Christian life implies the total consecration of all the possibilities of the body and of the soul in the service of God. Asceticism is neither an enslavement of the body nor a purely negative battle against raging passions, but the mastery over our psycho-physical nature with a view to putting it at the service of God. . . . Yoga, with its rich experience and its well thought-out technique can be of great help here."[2] The second example is taken from the work of King. It concerns the encounter between the Buddhist way of conceiving inter-subjective relations in the light of the principle of *anatta* or non-self, and the personalist way in which the Western Christian sees the precept of *agapé:* "For Christianity such a review of its own love policy, so to speak, in the light of the Buddhist witness would mean a reexamination of its hard aggressive personalism that tries too hard to be selfless and yet fears so much the loss of its own selfhood. . . . In losing contact with its own mystical depths, Christianity has made its love one-sided (hence not love) and lost that vital sense of Divine Presence upon which depend

[1] W. King, *Buddhism and Christianity* (London: G. Allen & Unwin, 1962), p. 173.
[2] J. Neuner (ed.), *Hinduismus und Christentum* (Vienna: Herder, 1962), p. 81.

the true depth and quality of Christian love even toward man." [3]
If it is true—and we have no doubt that it is—that the Christian
is interested in an encounter with non-Christian spiritualities,
even in the *quality* of its charity, then we have no further need
of proof: he needs this encounter just as he needs bread.

GENERAL BIBLIOGRAPHY

Cuttat, J. *La rencontre des religions.* Paris: Aubier, 1957.
Cornelis, E. *Valeurs chrétiennes des religions non-chrétiennes.* Paris:
Les éditions du Cerf, 1965
Dechanet, J. *La voie du Silence.* (coll. Voici), Plon.
Enomiya-Lassalle, H. *Zen—Weg zur Erleuchtung.* Wien: Herder, 1960.
Gardet, L. *Expériences mystiques en terres non-chrétiennes.* Paris: Al-
satia, 1953.
———*Thèmes et Textes mystiques: Recherche de critères en mystique
comparee.* Paris: Alsatia, 1958.
Hutten, K. *Die Bhakti-Religion in Indien und der christliche Glaube im
Neuen Testament.* Stuttgart: Kohlhammer, 1930.
King, W. *Buddhism and Christianity.* London: G. Allen & Unwin, 1962.
Kraemer, H. *Religion und christliche Glaube.* Göttingen: Vandenhoeck
& Ruprecht, 1959.
Lacombe, O. *Chemins de l'Inde et Philosophie chrétienne.* Paris: Alsatia,
1956.
de Lubac, H. *Aspects du Bouddhisme.* Paris: Les éd. du Seuil, 1951;
Zmida. Paris: Les éd. du Seuil, 1955.
Monchanin, J. and H. Le Saux. *Ermites du Saccidânanda.* Paris: Caster-
man, 1956.
Moore, C. (ed.). *Philosophy and Culture: East and West.* Honolulu:
Univ. of Hawaii Press, 1962.
Neuner, J. (ed.). *Hinduismus und Christentum.* Vienna, 1962.
Otto, R. *Mystique d'Orient et mystique d'Occident.* Paris: Payot, 1951.
Spencer, S. *Mysticism in World Religion.* Pelican Books, 1963.
Zaehner, R. *At Sundry Times.* London: Faber and Faber, 1958.

G. Neyrand/*Tokyo, Japan*

Christianity in Japan

"Quite often I feel a sudden urge to visit the universities of Europe, particularly the University of Paris. There, in the heart of the Sorbonne, I would cry out at the top of my lungs, like a man who has lost his senses, telling those who have more knowledge than desire to exploit it that their indifference causes a great number of souls to stray from the path of glory . . ." Everyone is familiar with these words of Francis Xavier written on January 15, 1544. When I was a seminarian about twenty years ago I believed that this cry was a sign of a period lacking missionary spirit, a period already past. I now think that the appeal of Francis Xavier has lost none of its immediacy in four centuries; it is to restate the very same thing in 1965 that I take up my pen today.

Japan: the Old and the New

Adaptation: leitmotif and charter of the mission; how certain is this? First, let us overlook the unpleasant connotation of the word "adaptation", tainted with condescension toward those who, of course, could never be like us. Let us clarify this. By adaptation I mean the act by which Christianity assists in the development of the civilizations which it meets. To the best of my knowledge, this idea is not found in tradition until the most modern times. Prior to the 20th century I know only of the let-

ter of St. Gregory the Great to St. Augustine of England. However, it is clear from the text that the pope, who in an earlier
letter had ordered the destruction of temples along with their
idols, reversed his decision and declared that, if the buildings
were sturdily constructed, it would be better to preserve the
temples and transform them into churches. As an example of
adaptation this one is indeed rather limited.

Although unrecorded in textual form, could adaptation have
been lived and practiced by the Church? Frankly, I find it difficult to quote a single historical example of adaptation. At
random, one might mention several sporadic examples such as
the bishops' miter, Roman law and Negro spirituals, but I
truthfully do not know of a single example of a non-Christian
civilization brought into bloom by Christianity.

There is, of course, the case of Greek culture. I shall not
approach the question of connections between Christianity and
Hellenism here. Let me say only that Christianity is difficult to
comprehend historically when considered independently of its
Greek heritage, and that one hardly can see how Christianity
could have brought Hellenism into bloom. Where is the Christian
Parthenon, the Christian Plato? In the history of Christianity,
it is its creative force which is far more striking than its fertility.
Christianity does not repair ruins; it builds anew. The Byzantine
cupola owes nothing to Phidias. Were not the Romanesque and
Gothic styles called precisely "The New West"?

Moreover, can one seriously imagine that Christianity could
be called to bring "pagan" civilizations into bloom? A "pagan"
civilization centers around a sovereign by divine right and a
lavish, refined elite who dominate a large slave class. There are
innumerable variants according to time and place, but the pattern is always the same. Now, to proclaim the lordship of Christ
in a divine-right monarchy is to shake the very foundation of
the kingdom. To proclaim that all men are brothers in a society
based on slavery, or at least on inequality among classes, is to
be, purely and simply, a revolutionary. To show that an idol is
nothing more than a statue is to kill the inspiration that created

it. No, it was no accident that the "good" emperors were the ones who ordered persecutions, nor that Christianity was accused of destroying the Roman Empire. Christianity is a terrible, destructive force. The Christian order is established following the liquidation of an ancient, non-Christian order.

The Japan born of the Meiji Revolution of 1868 was a completely new Japan. In undertaking this agonizing revision which opened the way to the Western world, there is no question that Japan had not deliberately sought this total break with the past. To preserve its genius, it had wanted only to master Western technology. From the West it wanted nothing but material force as a safeguard of its independence. But the race was a hard one, and the winner receiving the crown today finds himself a Westerner. The hundred years separating us from Meiji mark a span in Japanese history infinitely greater than the ten centuries of a very rich history that preceded it. This was indeed a total revolution, entailing the indissoluble acquisition of both Western science and Christian influence. Not that the promoters of the revolution had wanted to welcome Christianity; in fact, they were rather hostile to it. However, in accepting Western civilization they accepted in spite of themselves a Christian mentality in much the same way that Greece gave her spirit to her Roman conquerors.

Let us give some examples of this Christianization of modern Japan. Its present constitution, "imposed" by the Americans, is impregnated with the Christian spirit. Now, the Japanese find themselves very much at ease with this; if any of them wish it modified, it is not for this reason. The equality of citizens before the law (including the effective abolition of a titled nobility) is a matter of course. It is, however, the antithesis of the Tokugawa regime based upon strict maintenance of the social echelon inherited at birth. The present morality concerning marriage is in no way different from that current in the West. And yet only sixty years ago custom dictated that on January 1st a lawful wife must receive her husband's concubines and exchange trifling gifts with them. Unions and social security are on their way to reaching the level attained by these institutions in the West. In a word, the dignity of man is the foundation of their society.

Cannot Christian values be recognized in this fact? Some time ago, a draft of the Educational Charter was published under the auspices of the Department of Education. In this most interesting document, one thing is striking. In defining the type of man they wish to turn out, the authors avoid all expressions reminiscent of traditional Confucianism; instead, they speak of personality, liberty and love. These are terms that will not offend a single reader, yet, terms that have meaning only in their Christian context.

Let us consider another example. The weekly publication with the highest intellectual level and not at all suspected of having Christian leanings, very often treats matters concerning Christianity. And this is out of normal proportion to the small number of Japanese Christians. Besides, interest in Christianity is not aroused by the existence of a Japanese Church; rather, it is linked to an interest in things concerning the West. Christianity appears in Japan under the form of Western civilization.

The conclusion is obvious: the Japanese is not a "pagan"; he is a modern man. Totally different from his great-grandfather, he has rejected the gods, the ethics and the tradition of the latter. With largely Christian materials he has constructed a humanism that could almost be mistaken for the humanism of the West. However, one difference remains—if the Westerner, in so many instances, is no longer personally a Christian, the Japanese is not yet a Christian.

Christianity and the Japanese World-View

One Christian for every two or three hundred Japanese; one Catholic for every five hundred (a growth pattern which hardly exceeds that of the population); one practicing Christian out of three: this, to be blunt, is the situation. Why are there so few conversions? The answer is quite simple: there are few Christians because Christianity is not presented. But the question comes up again and it becomes necessary to look at things from a wider perspective.

No matter how Western and Christian today's mentality may be, the transformation is certainly far from complete. The difference between the Westerner who no longer has the faith and the Japanese who does not yet have it seems to me to be the difference between one who denies the absolute and one who does not know it. Ignorance of the absolute is one of the keynotes of the Japanese mentality.

The beautiful, for example, does not exist. No one contests the excellence of the Japanese in the realm of art, including the seventh art. One now finds no aesthetic theory among the Japanese. They calmly say that the beautiful is a subjective notion and that there is no reason to discuss it.

The idea of the beautiful in itself appears peculiar, but even more serious is the absence of absolute truth. All truth is relative to time and place and, above all, relative to the person expressing it; in other words, it is subjective. Holding an opinion has social significance (and, if need be, fulfills aesthetic functions) far more than having value as an expression of truth. The faith is a truth, so to speak, but a subjective truth, that is, it is a personal choice that would be unreasonable to force upon others. Has not one the right to prefer Picasso to Rouault and Bartok to Wagner? If there were an absolute truth in the realm of adventure, many different roads could lead there. What does it matter which way one chooses to climb Mount Fuji when all of them lead to the summit?

Moral obligation is also relative. It is not based on an absolute command of the conscience. It is a compromise between the desires of the heart and the order of the law. Moreover, the transcendental value of self remains shrouded in doubts, and suicide, that short cut to oblivion, is not necessarily an evil solution for a weary Sisyphus. There is no God, of course, and no afterlife, either. Now perhaps one might say: "It is exactly because there is no afterlife that one must live this one to its fullest." Let us not cry out too soon with sophisms, for so many people have no reason for living other than their pitiful faith in this passing world.

I ask students this question: "What do you think of this statement: 'All men are brothers'?" Their practically unanimous answer is: "Let's correct that sentence to read: 'All men must become brothers'." This correction is significant. They proceed from a metaphysical statement to a moral precept which is, moreover, considered right.

In this way, while a casual glance at daily life reveals no specifically Japanese traits, a deeper look shows that opinions are not measured by Western standards. In Japan the relative does not imply the absolute, nor the imperfect the perfect, nor one truth *the truth*. Man is definitely confined in the sphere of changing things. Such a rejection of the metaphysical leads, by a logical inversion, to the placing of a greater value on the things of this ephemeral world. The love of an uncertain world, of its very uncertainty, has led Japan to a refinement of social life that gives it great charm. Everything is bound up in nuances. The shimmering of a piece of silk, the insertion of an honorary particle in a name—these are the marks of a subtle scale of values. It is not a question of mincing words but of giving birth to resonance, even of expressing an instant's emotion in a poem of seventeen syllables.

Perhaps what I have just said is already a thing of the past. Science opposes fugitive truth with its solid certainties, certainties so sure that scientific truth becomes the only objective truth. Science has certainly brought a good measure of scientism to Japan, but above all it has brought the idea of objective truth. This tremendous benefit may well make up for some of the ill effects of scientism.

I would now like to consider the major obstacles encountered by a Japanese on the road to Christianity. The first problem is that Christianity is classified as a religion. Beneath this apparent tautology lies a strong element of scorn.

Does the comparative study of religions make sense? I have

my doubts. Would it not make the concept of religion purely equivocal? The closer one examines the essence of each religion, the more evident its fundamental originality becomes. If the extension of the concept of religion may be applied to many, then from a comprehensive perspective the common essence seems to disintegrate into contraries.

Whatever the case may be in the comparative study of religions, one must recognize that the word used to translate "religion" in Japanese connotes an idea totally different from the one which we understand by this word. For the contemporary Japanese the word does not express a concept; rather, it evokes a series of frankly unpleasant images.

First of all, a religion implies the existence neither of God nor of a god; it is above all a state of mind. That this state of mind may in fact correspond to reality is a secondary if not irrelevant consideration. The idea may be carried to an extreme: "That God exists or does not exist has no importance. If the believer is content with his faith, everything is perfect." Obviously, few would phrase it so starkly, but the very fact that some do demonstrates the tendency.

With such a state of mind as its essence, religion would seem something alienated from the world of reality, something useful for the weak, but in any case a remedy better ignored. At any rate, it implies a choice that emphasizes individual taste and precludes any idea of an apostolate. On the other hand, this faith-refuge disregards what our contemporaries hold most dear: building together the new world of tomorrow.

Such are the reactions ordinarily provoked by the word "religion". Are these reactions in fact particularly Japanese? In France some say: "Religion? That's folklore." Do not those who wish to be "honest before God" say comparable things? This is the problem: is religion a state of mind, and is the "religious" sphere a separate realm? If so, the modern world can only detest such a religion. If not, we must revise this "religious" category if we wish at least to use it in speaking of Christianity. J. P. Audet has written some very interesting material about this topic, emphasizing the excesses of the famous book by R. Otto. The "holy" must not be confused with the "sacred". "Sacred" is the opposite of "profane", while "holy" embraces both "sacred" and "profane". This is what is meant by saying that religion sanctifies *all* human activity. It is beyond categorization, concerning itself with scientific and economic progress, as well as literary and artistic achievement. Furthermore, Christianity brings the irrational-sacred element within the strict limits of the sacraments. The extension of the sacred into a broad sacral zone is a distortion of Christianity. We must not rebuild the courts of a temple whose veil has been rent.

Is it necessary to reject the pejorative term "religious" in Japan? Not necessarily, for the mentality there is quickly evolving. To many of today's Japanese, "religion" means something above all Christianity (a fact that proves Buddhism's loss of vitality). In this case, to say that Christianity is not a religion would lead to confusion. We find ourselves in the midst of an evolution.

Another obstacle confronting the Japanese of good will is the fact that Christianity is not presented. Let us put things back into their proper perspective. As everyone knows, Japan has completely succeeded in its efforts at Westernization in the scientific realm. Likewise, she compares favorably with Europe in medicine and law. The study of foreign languages, however, is far from reaching a desirable level, and the development of philosophy is very slow. If one were to consider Christianity as a single current of thought among many, he would realize that it is treated in a manner no worse than, for example, Marxism or existentialism. Certainly, in every instance, the basic works have been translated, but these translations, even if they do not contain grave misinterpretations—which unfortunately abound —seldom convey the spirit of the thinkers.

One more point must be emphasized: does Japan look to the West for knowledge and not wisdom? Is this the effect of an education grounded until recently in the knowledge of a certain number of linguistic characters? Whatever it may be, professors are not accustomed to encourage opinions among their students; they are content at times to present a very profound body of knowledge without conveying a value judgment. This erudite attitude does not lend itself to deep understanding of an author and to an accurate transposition of his work into Japanese.

Moreover, Japanese is one of the most difficult of languages. Classical in the year 1000, it has undergone a prodigious transformation since Meiji when it suddenly found the need to express all of modern culture. If the creation of a word to signify a concrete object like "necktie" or "artificial satellite" is simple, the transposition of the notion of "person" or "incarnation" is achieved only with the greatest difficulty. Furthermore, I wonder if the Japanese language, subjected for a hundred years to such amplification accompanied by drastic simplification, has not reached the limit of its potential. Perhaps it is out of breath. But I will turn from this technical problem, repeating only that the barrier raised by the Japanese language is much more serious than the multitude of translations would lead one to think.

A Japanese, admitting that Christianity (religion or not) has a value, resigned to the fact that the translation of the Bible is mediocre and Christian literature of little interest, encounters a new obstacle in his path: the division among Christians. There are Protestants (with sixty denominations), Catholics, Anglicans, and even Orthodox; each group has its own customs, its own exclusiveness—a scandal in the strongest sense of the word, a stumbling block for which the Japanese are certainly not responsible.

A Japanese now faces another obstacle. He is attracted to Christ, but it seems to him that seeking Christ's protection would be to deny himself, to deny the prerogative of man to solve his own problems. Baptism is a resignation. As for the rest, he need only observe gloomy gatherings of Christians to get the feeling that they are cowards who have given up trying to get along by themselves. This objection reminds me of a question that won recent renown: "Has Christianity robbed man of his virility?" I do not recall the answer given, and I am not sure whether or

not this is due to a simple lapse of memory. No, the problem is
not a new one, nor is it Japan's alone. To point out, among the
rare Christians, those who are even rarer, those whom one may
classify as dynamic, is perhaps a good *ad hominem* answer. But
an adequate answer, that is, a clearly defined theology of grace,
is not easy to provide.

The Possibility of Apologetics

I have said that Christianity is not presented. But one asks:
"What, then, is the Church doing?" Let us consider the situation
from the Church's viewpoint. The Church in Japan is not very
different from the Church in Europe of several years or several
decades ago. Organized into dioceses and parishes, she concentrates the bulk of her efforts upon the care of her faithful flock,
with the instruction of some catechumens added on like a precious ornament. This does not reflect upon the personal zeal of
Japanese or foreign priests. Considering the existing structure of
the Church, the distribution of duties, the formation in seminaries and the means of apostolate, they could hardly be otherwise.
Insofar as the proclamation of Christ to non-Christians is not the
central preoccupation of the Church, it is difficult to speak of a
missionary apostolate. In the age of great industrial enterprise
the Church is still in an artisan stage.

The poignant question of the very essence of the apostolate
arises long before organizational problems. No longer does anyone consider the apostolate to be an effort aimed at saving souls
from hell; this is most fortunate. Many think of counting bap-
tisms as if it were a question of recruiting the members of a sect;
this is not satisfactory. Many Christians are paralyzed in their
apostolate by what I call the alms complex wherein the Christian
who is rich in grace extends a generous hand to the poor pagan
deprived of spiritual riches. No self-respecting soul wishes to be
either the rich man who lets his alms fall from on high or the
humble one who stoops to pick them up. Such a complex must
be abandoned; if anyone gives, it is Christ alone, and if anyone
receives, it is each one of us, freely accepting a gift. Further-

more, the gift is not an exterior one, but rather a personal awakening to the truth, the objective truth which is valuable for whoever receives it, whether he recognizes it as such or not. Here I can only point out, without going into detail, the need for a theology of the apostolate. Let me repeat the definition of it given by Saint Paul: to proclaim to the Gentiles the boundless riches of Christ.

To present Christianity means first of all to present Christ himself. But where can one find a reliable, readable life of Christ for the non-Christian? The honorable exegetes have declared loud and clear that it is impossible to write a life of Christ. And if a courageous layman should undertake this task, he incurs the wrathful attention of the honorable theologians. Must we then condemn Renan?[1] A book like Blinzler's on the Passion[2] sets the course. But it is not enough to guarantee the historicity of the end of the Gospel and to consider the Gospel of the Infancy as *midrash*. It is the interval, with its miracles and difficult *logia*, which we would like to see explained. What *did* happen on the shore of the Sea of Galilee or on Mount Tabor? A Japanese professor asked this question: "If someone had taken a photograph when the resurrected Christ appeared to the apostles, would the film have recorded him or not?" I leave to my readers the chore of replying.

Today we like to present Christianity as salvation history. This is without a doubt an excellent dogmatic presentation, but to my mind it does not seem to be a very good introduction to Christianity. First of all, the idea of history in the fullest sense of the word is precisely a product of Christianity; the notion that history has a meaning is therefore not held in Japan. Next, the word "salvation" implies, at least in Japanese, the idea of escaping from a danger. Modern men do not generally feel lost; they hardly feel a need to be saved. Must we then begin by convincing them of their wretched condition as sinners in order to

---

[1] E. Renan, *Vie de Jesus* (Paris, 1863).

[2] J. Blinzler, *Der Prozess Jesu* (Regensburg: Verlag Friedrich Pustet, [2]1960).

bring them salvation through Jesus Christ? To me this position seems neither biblical nor traditional. It is rather in the light of justification that one perceives the abyss of sin. Is not the insistence of Saint Paul and the councils on the word "justification" significant? Should it not lead us to speak of a goal to be realized by humanity instead of a salvation history?

In seeking ideas, which might facilitate bridging the gap between a modern culture and Christianity, one quite naturally considers freedom. St. Paul tells us that the Christian is free in relation to the law. Exactly what does this mean for men of our time? Is the Christian exempt from all law? If so, why does he seem so hemmed in by commandments? Would we not have to say that with regard to the future he is freed from fate and with regard to the past he is freed from all his sins? In other words, he freely constructs his own life. But here we find ourselves far from Paul's idea of liberty considered in relation to the law of circumcision!

Need I discuss the liturgy? Certainly, since it is currently a popular topic, and since people wish it to be renewed. The most important considerations, from a missionary point of view, are funerals and weddings, since at each of these ceremonies eighty percent of those present are non-Christians who have perhaps never before entered a church. I believe that funerals and weddings are received quite well in Japan. Christian burials, despite an element of strangeness for the people, give rise to a surge of hope through which they easily surpass the traditional, but empty ceremony of the Buddhist *bonze* which conveys only total despair. As for marriages, the Shinto ceremony seems antiquated, and the lack of any ceremony at all leaves one dissatisfied. The Christian ceremony, both solemn and eloquent, is so fully satisfying that many non-Christians wish to be married in church.

The Mass itself interests only the small flock of the faithful. One cannot imagine that the inadequacies of the Latin Mass could hold the slightest appeal for the Japanese. The splendid liturgy of the Olympic Games demonstrated their superiority in this realm. By comparison, the translation of the Roman Mass appears to be a ridiculously insufficient effort. As a final remark on the liturgy, I shall quote these words as they were spoken by a catechumen who had just attended Mass: "They distribute the eucharist as if to dogs!"

I find myself in an apologetic position, but leading non-Christians to Christ entails the practice of apologetics. I realize that it has a bad press, but the scorn shown for apologetics in the West is perhaps not without harmful consequences in the missionary world. The "grounds for belief"—how old-fashioned that sounds! And yet is it not unreasonable to think that one isolated Christian among two hundred non-Christians (the Diaspora!) can live his faith without a solid foundation? And is it not presumptuous to think that a holy missionary, by his presence alone, will inspire acts of faith? Let us be honest. On any level, one believes something because it is true and because there are sound reasons to believe that it is true. (I need not explain that I am not seeking to prove the truths of faith but of establishing grounds for belief.)

I repeat, we need an apologetic. I would propose a study of the Christian phenomenon, to borrow Teilhard's term, showing the power of Christian activity in the course of history. I have already alluded to the destructive and constructive powers of Christianity. It is along these lines that an effective apologetic might be formulated. I repeat: it is the power of Christianity that must be considered and not simply the force of the visible Church. I was most pleased by a sentence I found in a recent book concerning the concept of progress: "The Gospel is infinitely more than the historical record of an ecclesial group." The influence of the Christian phenomenon on the progress of the world must be made clear. For example, can one affirm, or rather prove the following theses: the idea of progress is a Christian idea; it originates in Christianity which alone can justify it; the societies that have not known Christianity were all based on slavery or inequality among classes; Christianity alone leads to the realization of the brotherhood of man (Bergson's thesis);

Christian martyrs by far surpass all other martyrs both in number and quality; democracy is a product of Christianity and is
inconceivable without the existence of God. I propose these
theses without proposing an answer, for not only have I no answer but neither do I know where I could look for one.

Three Proposals

The preceding views rest on an opinion based on facts. I do
not pretend to justify this opinion, but it is time to make it
clearer. I will express it in three proposals.

First of all, I do not believe in the future of the "old Japan",
but I do believe in that of modern Japan, the Japan of transistors
and the monorail. By "old Japan" I mean the Japan of Buddhism,
including the "Zen" school, of Shinto shrines with their imme-
morial *torii,* the poetic Japan of Basho, the medieval [Japan] of
"Harakiri" or of "The Rain and Moon Tales", the Japan of flow-
ers, of kimonos, of the pigtail and of the tea ceremony. It is not
that these things are not infinitely fascinating, nor that they have
failed to give an exquisite expression of beauty. The old Buddhist temple or the Shinto high-place, inseparable from the noble
purity of the Japanese countryside, express a harmony between
man and nature which is not a mere visual pleasure but an aesthetic of the soul. Among the statues of Buddha more than one
proclaims a mystical message that classifies it among mankind's
greatest masterpieces.

I do not say that Buddhism is dead in Japan, but I believe that
it has lost its soul. The temple has become a museum and the
statue of Buddha hears the clicking of cameras instead of prayers. One might say that this tradition has created a particular
Japanese spirit that can never die. One might concede that many
elements of the old Japan are dead, but that their legacy lives
on in the particular structure of a Japanese spirit which should
be Christianized. I encounter this type of thinking quite often.
I feel that the Meiji Revolution has failed to sever all the roots
sunk in the past and that modern Japan has kept certain modes
of thought inherited from old Japan, but I do not believe in any

unchangeable structure. I do not believe in a future for these vestiges of the past.

My conclusion is clear: it is not up to Christianity to Christianize these cultural elements. Although historical study does have its own value, the task of Christianity is, above all, a work of creation in a modern world. Let us not fall back into neo-Gothic error. The true heir of Gothic style was Perret with his church at Raincy.

Secondly: I believe that the Church—and, more generally, Christianity—can and should open up to the modern world. John XXIII has given us the hope that this is indeed conceivable and feasible. Opening up to the world implies participation in the building of modern society. It is not a question, of course, of recreating a Christendom. No longer does the Church have to build and bless schools, hospitals or asylums. But it should be dynamically present in social promotion as well as in economic evolution. Such spiritual presence entails a minimum of structural organization combined with a maximum of creative energy.

For this, a spirituality addressing itself to the sanctification of the profane is necessary, but not sufficient. It is in the very structure of the society which is the Church that the desire to open up to the world should appear. This calls for radical reform. For example, it is a well-known fact that the apostolate is incompatible with the spirit (one can easily come to an agreement with the letter) of canon law. But we must go much further. There is, for example, by right, an incompatibility between the practice of religious vows and the missionary apostolate, whatever may be in fact the prevailing *modus vivendi*. The religious who steps beyond the limits of time is immediately situated in eschatology; this legitimate and admirable effort cannot be confused with the work of the sower of God's Word in this world.

Moreover, the poignant problem of the missionary must be considered: a priest's consecrated character separates him from the world; the layman lacks both competent formation and the necessary tools for action. One may ask, what about Catholic Action? Occasionally we hear of its failure and quite often of its crises. This makes it difficult to see it as a panacea; the hybrid solution of a worker-priest or of a lay member of a secular institute is an example more admirable than imitable. We must, I believe, reconsider the distinction between clergy and laity. Is it essential to the Church? Is it inconceivable that laymen might organically direct the apostolate and even the activity of the clergy? The example of the deacons in ancient Rome makes us stop and think. These thoughts are, moreover, related to the previously mentioned distinction between sacred and profane.

The necessary apostolic effort of all Christians presupposes, in order to be realized, the introduction of democracy into the Church. Freedom of expression and criticism, participation in decisions by vote, publication of debates, doing away with secrecy, normal accession to responsibility given to all Christians —such are the conditions which to me seem necessary for an apostolate in the modern world. And I do not see why these conditions cannot be implemented.

My third proposal is this: I believe that the Japanese thirst for the absolute. I have said above that Japanese tradition entails a denial of the absolute, but I add now that the Japanese are fortunately dissatisfied with this situation. Some of them express their discontent openly, such as the young novelist K. Oi, whose youth "cheated" him out of experiencing the war. His novels resound with the regret of having missed the chance to become a hero. The thirst for the absolute is also expressed, in an indirect yet powerful manner, by that classic theme of Japanese literature, the vanity of this world. All Japanese literature, from its beginnings to our time, represents an effort to transform this tragic assumption into an artistic expression that makes it bearable. Before the Christian invasion, Japan could offer values which, if not truly absolute, could at least approach the absolute. Such were Confucian filial piety, confidence in Amida's grace, feudal fidelity to a sovereign. Old Japan lived by these values until the Western influx swept away this unsteady safeguard. Today the Japanese awakes to an empty sky and a mechanized world. In the prodigious Japanese dynamism there is, moreover,

an unquestionable spontaneity, a forward flight, a leap into the
world to build what seems to be a modern variant of Pascal's
diversion.

No, the new god called Democracy cannot satisfy the recep-
tive souls of our contemporaries. To tell the truth, there are only
two forces today that are capable of quenching men's thirst for
the absolute: nationalism and Christianity. In the absence of the
second, unknown or too remote, the Japanese lean toward the
first. It is indeed difficult to reckon the danger presented by Japanese nationalism. I personally think it is great. Of course, economic necessity compels Japan to leave the country open at least
to exterior commerce, but a simultaneous exclusion of universal
ideas is perfectly possible. It must be emphasized that for a Japanese to become a Christian means that his faith in Jesus Christ
must exceed his love for his country. During a period of calm
this requires no special effort. During a time of crisis this calls
for martyrdom. Am I mistaken? I am under the impression that
the precise position of a Christian nationalism has not been sufficiently explained by the Church. This is not, however, a new
problem.

Japan practices Western Christianity. It is certain that Christianity has played a role in the past, but is it still valuable? Can
it call the future its own? Japan asks these questions. The West's
answer does not appear clear. If a living, universal, modern
Christianity were presented to him, I am sure that the Japanese
would accept it without hesitation, for he is wonderfully generous. The preceding pages have set forth several opinions which
will, without doubt, give rise to criticism, but if there is one point
on which I would like to be believed, it is my affirmation that in
the Japanese heart there exists a boundless store of generosity.

PART II

BIBLIOGRAPHICAL
SURVEY

Agnes Cunningham, S.S.C.M./*Chicago, Illinois, U.S.A.*

Complexity and Challenge: The American Catholic Layman

On February 22, 1965 Canon Joseph Cardijn became a Cardinal of the Catholic Church. The significance of this event for American Catholics might have been overlooked—even by American Catholics—except for the fact that the same year (1965) marked the twenty-fifth anniversary in the United States of the Young Christian Students (YCS), begun at Notre Dame College (now, University) by Father Louis Putz, C.S.C. While it is true that the entire story of the Catholic layman in America cannot be told completely in terms of YCS, it is just as true that this movement (the word is stressed deliberately in the YCS *mystique*) is, perhaps, an ideal point of departure for a serious discussion of the complex, challenging phenomenon: the American Catholic layman. Whether considered in its historical relation to the American scene or in the unique quality of its structure, YCS has something to say about what the layman is and what, hopefully, he could be in a free, pluralistic society.

The Historical Situation

In 1940, American Catholicism stood in the full current of a new vitality of ferment and growth following the inauguration of what was later to be identified as the "age of the lay apostle". Earlier, Pius X had issued a call for apostolic laymen in every

111

parish. Identifying their proposed activity as "Catholic Action", he inaugurated programs of liturgical renewal and of religious formation—always with the layman in mind. Later, Pius XI indicated further implications of this "apostolate", encouraging its orientation toward social consciousness and the temporal order. The Catholic Church seemed to be in a position to translate into the American idiom the apostolic activity of the layman, outlined by the popes. For one thing, the day of "ghetto" Catholicism gave indications of being on the wane. For another, the stigmas attached almost from the beginning of the nation to "immigrant" Catholicism seemed capable, finally, of assimilation. Catholics, having proved their patriotism in war and their cooperation—if not significant contribution—in times of national stress, were forgiven for being Catholics and were accepted more and more as Americans.

The Unique Structure of YCS

Into this atmosphere YCS was introduced. The formula: *observe, judge, act,* had been initiated by Canon Cardijn with his first group of workers in Belgium. These elements, which St. Thomas considers as parts of the virtue of prudence,[1] constitute more than a mere formulation. They indicate a technique and a program. That they were later stressed by Pope John as the foundation of all activity in the lay apostolate came as a surprise to no one who had tried to integrate them into his experience of the Christian mystery.[2] The distance-in-involvement, the other-centered, situation-directed attitude necessitated by this basic method is one reason for its unique structure. Two other factors are its stress on the lay student's responsibility for initiative and thought and its emphasis on a preparation for group action. Out of the initial YCS group there came leaders for a subsequent movement of Young Christian Workers and members of the Christian Family Movement. The Fides Press was established to let people

[1] *Summa Theologiae,* IIa IIae, q. 48.
[2] Encyclical letter: *Mater et Magistra* (Glen Rock, N.J.: Paulist Press, 1961).

know what was being done. YCS was in the front lines. It seemed as if the laity were about to "arrive".

The Layman Revealed but not Realized

The plaint of the Catholic layman in the United States today, when carefully interpreted, is a plea for a position in the Church such as that supposed and envisioned by the ideals and purposes of YCS. Both the Greater Prophets and the Lesser call for a structure and a role in which the layman will be recognized admittedly and effectively as a mature, responsible member of the People of God. This position has not been achieved. Nor, it would seem, has it been granted. One group of students, twenty-five years ago, along with other groups similarly inspired "caught the vision". It would almost seem that the sole differentiating fact in today's picture is that a new generation has replaced the former. Must we, then, join forces with those who claim that "nothing has changed" for the layman in the Church? Is the "age of the lay apostle" actually destined to be an ever-recurring series of moments in cyclic time? Is the lay apostolate nothing more than a theological treadmill? In order to seek an approach to the response of Christian hope to such questions, we must ask others: Who is the American Catholic layman in late mid-20th century? What is expected of—and permitted—him as a member of the laity? From what sources does the inspiration of his activity, his action or, perhaps, his *activism* flow?

The Catholic Layman in the United States

The American Catholic layman is coming of age in the Church. One of the most certain signs is his experience of an "identity-crisis". A summary review of the bulk of articles and books devoted *to himself*—for the greater part *by himself*—reveals a rather tortured probing of the image to unveil the reality and of the reality to induce evolution to what still threatens to escape in symbol. At one level, the American Catholic layman is, in general, very like his lay-brothers all over the world, that is, he shares with them a certain character and, in consequence, a precise mission: "These faithful are by baptism made one body with Christ and are constituted the People of God; they are in their own way made sharers in the priestly, prophetical and kingly functions of Christ; and they carry out for their own part the mission of the whole Christian people in the Church and in the world."[3] In his awareness of the principles underlying this statement even before the Council fathers had proclaimed it, the layman in America has been asking for a more precise explanation of what is meant by "their own way" and "their own part". His frequent impatience and *malaise* touching the question of his membership in the Church in its practical dimensions mark his similarity, in particular, to other laymen in countries such as France and Germany where demands are also being made in the name of Christian adulthood.

Yet, for all his likeness to laity in the Church universal, the American Catholic layman is very unlike the rest of them. This is so because the Catholic Church in America is itself unlike the Church in any other part of the world. In the first place, the Church in the United States has never been monistic, triumphant, or formally persecuted. From the days of the Founding Fathers, Catholics had to learn to make their way in a pluralistic society where it was possible to survive but not to flourish, and where the primordial ideal of religious freedom was granted to them grudgingly in an atmosphere of, at times, hostile toleration. The Church has never lost ground in America because she could only gain ground. The story of her gradual "emergence from the ghetto" has been told elsewhere.[4] What has still to be told is the story of her adaptation to a society where individual liberty is advocated under often severe restraint from group-pressures, and where separation of Church and State is defended on the grounds of basic Christian principles in a "Christian" society.

It is not to be wondered at, then, if the American Catholic

[3] *Constitution on the Church* (Glen Rock, N.J.: Paulist Press, 1965), Art. 31.

[4] Daniel Callahan, *The Mind of the Catholic Layman* (New York: Scribner Library, 1963); T. McAvoy, *Roman Catholicism and the American Way of Life* (Notre Dame: Fides Publishers, Inc., 1960).

layman finds himself in a state of confusion. In the past, he sought defense and protection within the Church against the influences of Protestantism or Secularism; against Logical Positivism or Pragmatism; against technological or intellectual threats to his faith and his Church. Today, *if* he seeks, it is in the direction of dialogue: scientfic, humanistic, religious. Finding that he no longer looks out to the world because he is already there, he discovers multiple *"conditions de possibilité"* stretching out like so many crossroads before him. It is in this *milieu* that he undertakes the quest for self-identity, prefacing the question, "Who am I?" with the statement that he has something worth saying.[5]

There are, however, laymen who do not seek. An additional contributing factor to the confusion on the lay scene in America is that, just as all vocal laymen are not necessarily prophets, neither are all laymen by any means vocal. Non-vocal members of the laity are usually referred to as "apathetic", *apathy* being a very serious sin. It is precisely in their condemnation of the "passive" laity and by the attitude assumed in their regard that the "prophets" of the new age run the risk of failing to accomplish a mission they perceive quite clearly and of defeating in some measure the cause to which they have rightly dedicated themselves. "Anyone who speaks ecstatically does himself good," claims St. Paul (1 Cor. 14, 4) "but the inspired preacher (*prophēteuōn*) does a congregation good," that is, he ". . . encourages and comforts them" (1 Cor. 14, 3). The problem of clergy-lay tensions or of religious-lay divisions has tended to cloud the vision of those who might well examine lay-to-lay relationships with a view to an apostolate of educating, edifying (*aedificare*) and instructing at close range the many whose faith and charity have not yet awakened to the meaning of *community* nor reached out to the broad horizons of Christian liberty.

[5] Michael Novak, *A New Generation: American and Catholic* (New York: Herder and Herder, 1964); Donald Thorman, *The Emerging Layman* (New York: Doubleday and Co., 1962). Cf. also the select bibliography in *The Mind of the Catholic Layman, op. cit.,* pp. 200-3 for representative contemporary works.

The American Apostolate

Optimistic as is the project of achieving desired goals for the layman through the apostolate of like-to-like (another aspect of the YCS technique), it still remains that the Church in America in its institutional character is unquestionably and predominantly clerical. By this I mean, that he who thinks "Church" thinks: "Bishop—Priest—Religious". There is nothing within the present structure of the Church to permit responsible action on the part of the laity, according to the ideals and aims of the lay apostolate as it is being interpreted today by serious theologians, by knowledgeable members of the clergy and hierarchy. What is more significant is that no one seems to know exactly how to go about reaching these goals. The efforts of the layman who aspires to a "position and task of active co-responsibility and work inside and outside the Church",[6] and that by reason of his "sacramental consecration and empowerment", will very likely be *supervised* by clerical members. What he seeks and needs is to be *supported* and *sustained* by them. The dilemma, from the hierarchical point of view, seems to focus on the difficulty of incorporating the "enlightened" and of arousing the individualists or the indifferent, once these have been properly identified. When one surveys the apostolic endeavors in which the laity have been and are encouraged and permitted to engage, one can better understand the plight of the American layman and the perplexity of his bishop.

As far back as the present generation can remember, the principal, if not the sole, work of the laity was that of contributing generously (whether in terms of money or of personal service) to the Catholic school system. In the same tradition was included his participation in the various events through which financial aid is supplied to parochial and diocesan funds. A slightly different emphasis was given by those parish organizations in which temporal needs, social functions and religious devotions concur

---

[6] Karl Rahner, "Baptism, the Sacramental Basis of the Layman's Position in the Church," in *Nature and Grace* (New York: Sheed and Ward, 1964). Cf. also *Jubilee* 12 (April, 1964), pp. 6-11.

with amazing naïveté. These groups, within their limits, provide an outlet for the expenditure of time, talent and energy, and attempt to provide a certain mode of spirituality, often in terms of sacramental life. But none of this can be considered "active co-responsibility" for the layman seeking a genuine apostolate. Nor is he satisfied to be told it is so.

To find a line that runs more directly to the notion of an authentic apostolate, it is necessary to return once again to an examination of the 1940 era. Previous to this date and following it, an increasing number of organs for apostolic activity, both organized ("official") and spontaneous ("unofficial"), testified to the new understanding by priests and people of the layman's membership in the Church.[7] These beginnings were brave. Many of them have developed into movements that exist and are fruitful today either in themselves or in subsidiary groups. Some of them, certainly, will continue to contribute to the progressive evolution of the laity. The best of them, though, have found the leavening of the mass a slow, difficult process.

Strangely enough, the factor of localization has been one obstacle. Ideas originating in the Middle West, long recognized for its vitality and initiative in experimentation wth new forms of "witness", often meet a barrier of judgment directed against an area regarded elsewhere as socially, culturally, or educationally inferior. At times, growth was impeded by aberrations which simulated a valid structure but which ended in "activism" and falsified the concept of genuine activity. At other times, the tendency to "organize" produced such a proliferation of "ways and means" to exercise the apostolate that the apostolate itself too often became a matter of secondary importance.

There where the layman has been able to engage meaningfully and with liberty in an apostolic work that answers to his aspirations, another difficulty at times appeared. This was the experience of disillusionment. It has been known by many who gave

[7] Cf. Louis Putz, *The Modern Apostle* (Dome Book edition, 1964), pp. 41-102; *idem*, "The Apostolate," in *Perspectives* (Sept.-Oct., 1962); L. Ward, *Catholic Life, U.S.A.: Contemporary Lay Movements* (St. Louis, 1959).

themselves with devotion and enthusiasm to the promising means by which the layman would arrive at recognized maturity. They themselves were the first to be caught in the atmosphere of "adolescence" in which their commitment had been made. This is not to say they were immature, nor that the movements were conducive to maintaining immaturity. On the contrary, they were "apostles", recognized as being "ahead of the times", or "in advance of their years". They were, unfortunately, ahead of the bulk of the Catholic population. It was lack of comprehension and response within the Church who found herself face to face with what could easily be dismissed as the exaltation of a new *illuminati,* that often led to frustration and discouragement. Many of the laity eventually passed through the crisis of a decision challenged and reviewed realistically at the level of their own ontology. Their mature reaffirmation was more sober, it is true, but it was also more profound and more truthful, that is, in greater conformity with the reality of the layman's role as it actually exists until it can in time give way to a new dimension.

For the present, the forms taken by the apostolate are rapidly changing to meet new exigencies and follow new directions. The Sodality of Our Lady, for example, dedicated to forming an elite to a life of deep spirituality out of which a response to apostolic summons should ideally rise, has thought well, recently, to reassess its values. Increasing numbers of young men and women who feel moved to give something of them*selves* to Christ in his Church find opportunity for action on a limited time-basis (one year, renewable at will) in no-priest, no-nun areas of the United States through *Extension Lay Volunteers* (ELV). Membership in PAVLA (*Papal Volunteers for Latin America*) means a three-year term of activity in one of the Latin American countries, following an intensive program of training and preparation. These two groups have become the model for others similarly aimed at increasing the possibilities of the Christian witness in education programs, care of the sick, or social work. Each of them is intended to provide a means of entry into one or another aspect of the lay apostolate understood as service and commitment. All of them demand self-sacrifice, poverty, and the deferment of one's lifework during the time thus given to the Church. Centers such as the *Grail* in Loveland, Ohio and *International Catholic Auxiliaries* Training House in Evanston, Illinois are among those where a lifetime apostolate consists, precisely, in preparing others for the lay apostolate.

Among those who choose not to affiliate themselves with any established movement, a highly effective apostolate is exercised in almost as many fields as there are human occupations. Notable among these are the efforts of an increasing number of journalists and authors, lay-directed publications, and a few publishing houses which seem to be more sensitive than others to the possibility and the demands of apostolic orientation. Shops can be found across the country handling contemporary art pieces that are Christian at the same time that they are *good* art. Artists, encouraged by this incentive, are attempting to establish an "apostolate of the image" which has, at times, produced works worthy of approval on "religious", if not theological grounds.

While all that has been said in no way pretends to be an exhaustive statement on the lay apostolate in the United States, it is sufficiently representative to indicate the main trends of the overall situation.[8] What is being sought by the layman is involvement with the world in which he finds himself, that is, with a world in which as a Christian, he is increasingly inclined to *choose* to *be* and to *act*. In the light of this intuition, a number of questions come to mind. To what extent has the layman begun to investigate and purify the conflicting concepts of "apostolate" which he seems to harbor? Might he not, for example, study the relationship between apostolic situations which remove him from his *milieu* (social, cultural, economic) and those which insert him

[8] In an effort to avoid presumption, favoritism and publicity, no attempt will be made to identify the "hidden faces" in the preceding paragraph. For the benefit, however, of non-American readers, I will indicate the names of some writers and publications. Acquaintance with them will lead to knowledge of the rest: D. Callahan, J. G. Lawler, M. Novak (cf. *Concilium*, Vol. 1, 1965), P. Scharper, D. Thorman; *Commonweal, Continuum, Cross Currents, Jubilee, National Catholic Reporter, Perspectives.*

more deeply into it? To what degree is the "new image" of the layman in the Church interpreted or betrayed by contemporary developments in the apostolate? Does the intensive, temporary program foster or hinder a continued, authentic orientation towards lay action after return to the "normal" life-situation? Should the premise of a "structured" apostolate along lines now familiar to us be challenged? Are the difficulties between hierarchy-clergy and laity the result, at a very profound level, of conflicting structures *on both sides?*

Such questions can be answered best by the layman himself and he is, in fact, moving toward a more thorough investigation of the conditions out of which they rise. However, an adequate examination of the structure and elements of his apostolate must be situated in interiority. In other words, that which is external to him must be incorporated into the mystery which is the principle and essence of his activity. At this point, we turn to consider what was called earlier the "source of his inspiration", his spirituality.

Spirituality of the American Layman

Among those who discuss the spirituality of the layman, there are some who claim that none exists—nor, do they say, has it ever. The layman's own demand for an "authentic lay spirituality" seems to confirm this point of view.[9] In response to his request, "spiritual writers" (the term can be ambiguous) are producing books and articles—some good, others more or less enlightened. One characteristic common to many of these is a determined effort to demonstrate that "there is no essential difference between the holiness of the layman and the holiness of the religious". It might be remarked, in passing, that such an assertion is consoling for religious. Time after time, the choice items on publishers' lists are headed, "Lay Spirituality" or are directed "to the (lay) Christian in the modern world". For the layman

---

[9] Cf. Callahan, *op. cit.,* p. 116.

who is attempting to distinguish himself from clerical and religious Christians, the claim can be embarrassing.[10]

The question, "Does a lay spirituality exist?" presupposes at least two other questions: first of all, by "lay" spirituality does one understand spirituality *of* the layman or spirituality *for* the layman? Secondly, presuming its existence, does "lay" spirituality differ from any other type of spirituality, and if so, how does it differ? Certainly a spirituality *of* the layman does exist, that is, the American layman, like any other, has been incorporated into the People of God, has been inserted into Christ. He lives with the life of the indwelling Trinity. "God's love has been poured forth in our hearts by the Holy Spirit who has been given us" (Rom. 5, 5).

A spirituality *for* the layman is another matter. From this point of view, "spirituality" must be considered as a corporate personality, a universal mode, a communal manner of existing proper to the layman given his position and role in the Church. It must be available to all, yet in no way violate the specific individuality of each one. "We have gifts that differ with the favor that God has shown us," says St. Paul (Rom. 12, 6). Echoing his thought, Gerard Manley Hopkins, the English convert Jesuit, wrote:[11]

> Christ plays in ten thousand places,
> Lovely in limbs, and lovely in eyes not his
> To the Father through the features of men's faces.

An appropriate spirituality of this kind does not exist. Inability to find has led the layman to seek.

Inasmuch as every man is Christ to the Father, as the poet says,

---

[10] The "definition by negation" of the laity as "non-clerical members of the faithful" has been modified by Vatican Council II to "all the faithful except those in holy orders and those in the state of religious life specially approved by the Church", in *The Constitution on the Church* (Art. 31).

[11] Gerard Manley Hopkins, *Poems* (London: Oxford University Press, 1930).

favored with the same grace in variety of gifts, according to the apostle, "there is no essential difference between the holiness of the layman and the holiness of the religious". However, the grace —the life—of God is not a form superimposed upon human nature. Rather, it penetrates, expressing itself through the "shape" of the vessel it fills, to use a scriptural metaphor. It effects transformation according to the particularity of each individual and in this sense the "holiness"—the spirituality—of the Christian whose vocation in the Church is to be there as a layman will, by reason of his being and his mission, differ from the holiness of the Christian who is a cleric or a religious. The Christian life and holiness have their roots in the same soil. The manner in which each plant assimilates nourishment and changes air, water, minerals into its unique type of beauty will vary. Put another way, Christian spirituality, even in being a matter of *community,* is individualized—but never individualistic.

One heartening sign of the "search for spirituality" is the layman's interest in theology. European theologians who are expressing their thoughts on a theology of the laity especially attract him. Because of satisfaction or dissatisfaction (as the case may be) with required theology courses, students in Catholic Colleges are turning to summer or full-time course work in graduate theology programs now being offered at a number of Universities. Nor is this true only of Catholic College students. Some of this training is put to practical use either in parish CCD (Confraternity of Christian Doctrine) classes or in College Theology Departments, where increasing numbers of lay professors are being employed. More importantly, there seems to be a definite growth from pietism to *Pietas* as a result of the serious, vibrant confrontation of revelation under the action of the Spirit of Christ.

Influences which have formed and nourished the spiritual life of the American layman have, on the whole, tended to overlook the action of the Holy Spirit. Heir to a strong tradition of Jansenism (from France *via* Ireland), American Catholicism has long been marked by a juridical approach to religious practices, a legalistic interpretation of the commandments and church law, a tendency to minimize the Fatherhood of God. Contact with early Puritanism served only to emphasize these traits. America is known throughout the world for its sacralization of the letter of the law. Equally as dominant is the emphasis on the need for strong "will power" to overcome the sinful weakness of human nature, often accompanied by stress on both the binding force and the intrinsic value of *duty*—strange echo in this ensemble of a Kantian theme.

Unlike European Jansenism, which kept the unworthy faithful at a distance from God, the American version resulted in a veritable eucharistic triumph. This was due to pastors of dioceses and parishes who, undisturbed by the scrupulous practice of confession-before-communion, hoped that the phenomenal number of communicants was matched by a depth and quality of devotion. The sincere desire for renewal of life and growth in holiness accounts, also, for the large numbers of lay people who make closed retreats, some of them annually. Given one or another area of the country, there can be found concentration on parish missions, confraternities, third orders, cursillos. Reactions for and against such practices depend to such a marked degree on subjective judgments that it is impossible to evaluate definitively their objective contribution to a spirituality of the layman. At times, they seem to foster *devotions* rather than *devotion*, to lag behind biblical and liturgical renewal, to encourage dependency upon a mediation as upon an absolute, thus impeding growth in liberty to the "full measure of development found in Christ" (Eph. 4, 14).

A very significant factor in the question of the layman's spirituality is an influence that is scarcely ever mentioned. This is the "training" or, perhaps, more happily the *experience* of life in a seminary or novitiate. There have always been Catholic men and women who, after a given length of time in one of the stages preparatory to the religious life, have come to the decision that their vocation lies elsewhere. Over and above this, one of the most critical problems faced by religious orders and congrega-

tions in the United States at the present time is that of member-
withdrawal, sometimes after many years of religious life. This is
not the place to initiate a discussion of a problem that has yet to
be treated justly and humbly from many points of view. It is not
out of place, however, to indicate here that not a few lay men
and women learned to "put down roots" in a life of apostolic orientation after a situation of withdrawal from a world to which
they later returned. It is not to be wondered at, if some of the
most constructive criticism in the Church today is being offered
by those who saw archaic structure and traditionalistic "red-
tape" at close range. The layman whose road to the apostolate
has detoured through a novitiate or seminary has a unique contribution to make to the lay world, it would seem. What he has
seen should increase his awareness of the human element capable
of betraying an ideal at any level of dedication. It may help him
to be more patient with reform that is needed in the Church,
when it is introduced more slowly than he would like. Quite
possibly, it might become a factor in the development of *his*
spirituality.

Conclusion

In the light of a Silver Jubilee, we began this discussion of the
American Catholic Layman. Considered in himself, in his apostolate, or in the spirituality which he seeks while striving to live
it, he is complexity and challenge to himself, as well as to the
Church. He is the first to realize that it is more than time to face
the challenge and penetrate the complexity.

It is not necessary that the identity-crisis of the American layman continue indefinitely. For many reasons, America is the best
place for the greatest possible development of the new concept
of the layman in the Church. So many obstacles that exist elsewhere have never been a factor to be considered in the United
States. The lack of a long historical tradition is an advantage, in
this case: there is very little terrain that has to be cleared away
to permit a "fresh start". Quite possibly, the solution is as simple

as a four-word motto which he has surely heard repeatedly: *Become what you are.*

Complexity in the apostolate rests, as we have seen, on the nature and number of structures already existent and rapidly multiplying. In his own challenge of ecclesiastical structure, he would do well to examine those of his own making. To the extent that any apostolic movement becomes a kind of *Linus's blanket,* enfolding in security a liberty summoned to move ahead, it will add to the confusion and destroy its own *raison d'être.*

In an assessment of his "spiritual life", the layman must, first of all, count the strengths that are already his. One of these, certainly, is his relationship—for lack of a more specific word—to the eucharist. If the liturgical reform and renewal launched by Vatican Council II can progress to a stage of effective pedagogy in the Christian Life, the layman's devotion can become the basis for an understanding and participation in the eucharist as a sacrificial-memorial meal shared in *community.* This experience will, in turn, become the means of purifying and refining the sense of eucharistic "devotion" among the laity. So, too, it would seem that the Lay Retreat Movement, in the measure that it can respond to the actual needs and aspirations of the layman, not situating him toward monasticism but in the midst of the world which is his mission, will also contribute to the evolution of an authentic spirituality.

Somewhere along the way, the American layman ought to be guided in his reading of the "new theology". Ideally, this should be one of the areas where members of the clergy would take their places with the laity in the People of God. There is much that is presumed as already known in the reflections of contemporary theologians, especially on the European scene, where the living tradition is situated in a sense of history, of the primitive Church, of the Greek and Latin Fathers of the Church. These are elements lacking, to a great extent, even in the best of the theology programs actually being offered in the United States. Without this foundation to speculative theological thought, there is danger of imprecision or imbalance in formulating an opinion (in the strict sense of the word) or stating a conclusion.

Guidance is needed, too, for the interpretation of orientations in theological thought that has resulted from dialogue with Existentialism, Phenomenology, Personalism, Marxism. True, these influences have begun to penetrate the climate of American intellectual life, but while the use of these words and their particular vocabularies have become clichés in many circles, their significance and implications remain esoteric.

Finally, the layman in the world must learn to balance (not resolve) the tension between the eschatological and the incarnational aspects of his apostolate. If it is true that through the adult, responsible living of the Christian mystery, confusion can be transformed into meaningful paradox, the layman who has tried to grow to adulthood in the Church must be hopeful. It is to be ardently desired that before another twenty-five years have passed, he will be able to answer the summons proclaimed in Leviticus: "You must hallow the fiftieth year, and proclaim liberty throughout the land to all its inhabitants; it is to be a jubilee for you, when each of you shall return to his own possessions" (25, 10). The "possessions" are identified for the layman by St. Paul: ". . . the world, life, death, the present, the future—all of it belongs to you. But you belong to Christ, and Christ belongs to God" (1 Cor. 22, 23).

Christian Duquoc, O.P./*Lyons, France*

The Believer and Christian Existence in History

Since the appearance of Father Congar's monumental work, *Jalons pour une théologie du laïcat*,[1] the number of books and reviews on the subject of the laity has steadily increased.[2] There can be no question here of reviewing them, or even of listing the titles. It is enough to mention the fact; their number will prove their significance. The layman is no longer, according to the formula of Leo XIII, "he who, in the Church, obeys and honors the clergy".[3] He is entitled not only to receive the sacraments and to hear the authentic Word of God, but also to contribute his views in the formulation of Church policy. This new position held by the layman, his awareness of his rights in the Church, has been and still is the source of a great number of movements uniting the laity to witness to the inspired testimony of the Christian in the world.

[1] Y. Congar, Eng. ed.: *Lay People in the Church* (Westminster, Md.: The Newman Press, 1965).

[2] Cf. *Laïcs et Mission de l'Eglise* (*Lum. et Vie* nn. 63, 65) (Lyons, 1963).

[3] Leo XIII, *Letter to Monseigneur Meignan, Archbishop of Tours.* We cite the text: "It is established and manifest that there are in the Church two orders by nature distinct: the pastors and the flock, that is to say, the leaders and the people. To the first order belongs the function of teaching, of governing, of directing men's lives, of imposing rules on them; the other has the duty of being submissive to the former; of obeying, of executing orders, and of rendering it honor." (Dec. 17, 1888, cited in *The Laity, a Collection of Pontifical Teachings*, edited by the Monks of Solesmes (Paris: Desclée et Cie, 1956), §§142, 106.

These movements are extremely different one from another: they extend from the closest relationship with the hierarchy, such as the structure of French Catholic Action, to a very pronounced autonomy. Moreover, the disappearance of temporary functions taken over by the Church—the investigation of denominational institutions whose aims are purely temporal—influence the laity to form new and different ties with the hierarchy, with various business and political associations which are, in fact, neither commanded by their faith nor demanded by the hierarchy.

This new situation, developing without plan, provokes tensions: pastoral and sociological tensions are best known because they are visible. Everyone knows of the split among Catholics in France, played up as they are by a press that thrives on controversy. These discussions have theological repercussions, and theology runs the risk of becoming the supposedly rational justification of behavior which has an unacknowledged emotional basis. There are, no doubt, other tensions less well known, although some hints concerning them reach us through the spiritual writings of Teilhard de Chardin and commentaries on them. These tensions belong to a more spiritual order: they testify to an uprooting and doubt concerning faith as lived at this time. Until now the different schools of spirituality have proposed methods; they are, rightly or wrongly, considered inadequate. Accused of having been conceived by monks or clerics for monks and clerics, there is a suspicion that (more or less consciously) they attempt to identify Christian life and religious life. All that was well and good when the laity had neither a special mission of its own nor a mission in the Church—a position that no longer has any justification, if the laity is fully in the Church. There is a certain manner of acting which, although of the world, is no less bound by the demands of the Gospel, and the layman would not be able to live these demands like a monk or a religious: he would then tend to deny his authentic insertion in the world.

Teilhard de Chardin's book, *The Divine Milieu*,[4] is born of

---

[4] P. Teilhard de Chardin, *The Divine Milieu* (New York: Harper, 1960); *idem, Hymn of the Universe* (New York: Harper & Row, 1965).

such preoccupations. By his profession, Teilhard passed his life as a seeker, whose passion for knowledge of the cosmic dynamism was something essential. He undertook to rethink in new categories the old sayings of the great spiritual writers (intuitions that had not lost their value) and the unchanging evangelical requirements. But for modern man they take on a rhythm in the renewed dynamism which will lead him to exploration, to knowledge, to the transformation of this world, to the building of social structures, to the elimination of certain forms of individualism. The Christian will give ultimate meaning, by identification with the historic passion and resurrection of Jesus Christ, to the already existing dynamism which is full of meaning, and to which he cannot refuse to devote himself without losing his humanity and without denying the ultimate Christian meaning of this world.

Father de Lubac[5] has vigorously emphasized the traditional aspect of Teilhard's thought. It shocked many minds not trained to unify their human life (as it becomes part of the general movement which envelops it), and their Christian conduct. The latter had only too often neither a social nor a cosmic aspect. The practical and spiritual conduct of the Christian layman relied less on revelation and hope in the passion and resurrection of Christ than on marginal benefits. Spirituality requires all kinds of centers, but many of them may become deviations from the center of the Christian mystery. The conjoined efforts of liturgical and biblical reviews progressively organizing the liturgy around Christ as center have led to a more authentic perception of the original unity of all Christian spirituality. Consequently it concerns itself with the sanctity of the "People of God", with the "perfection to which they are called".[6]

Without doubt there still remains an acute sense of what is distinctive in certain situations facing Christians today: the

[5] H. de Lubac, *La pensée religieuse de Père Teilhard de Chardin* (Paris: Aubier, 1962); *idem, La Prière du Père Teilhard de Chardin* (Paris: Artheme Fayard, coll. Le Signe, 1964).

[6] Dom Lafont, *La Sainteté du peuple de Dieu* (Ed. La Pierre qui vire, 1964).

attention given to marriage, for example, shows how profound a concern of modern sensibility it is.[7] But no one dreams, while stressing the importance of the immediate situation for the Christian mystery, of isolating it from the center which gives it value. A married layman, a priest, a single woman, a workman, an engineer, a professor—they are in different situations that urge them to live Christianity in their own unique way. It remains true, however, that modern authors insist on an attitude of faith as a common foundation for Christian life, no matter in what situations Christians may find themselves and whatever be the spiritual school they accept, whether by inclination or education.[8] And here, an attitude of belief must not be understood as a situation without an objective aspect: faith is explicitly faith in Jesus Christ in the fullness of his redemptive and cosmic mystery.[9] It is then apparent after a glance at contemporary literature that the emergence of the laity in the Church is accompanied by their will to understand spirituality as no longer detached from the heart of faith, but as the most integral, personal expression of their existence in the total mystery of Christ.

In France, Catholic Action, by its method of revision of life, that is to say, by its effort to discern Christ's action in the present day, has helped not a little to orient lay Christians and their priests toward the center of their faith, and to outline a Christian way of life that is new and closely linked to the structures most central to faith.[10] This effort is supported by the periodical journals: we shall name only the two expressing the principal French opinions: *La Vie Spirituelle* and *Christus*. The former, significantly enough, has tried to concentrate the theme of its

---

[7] We refer here especially to the enterprises undertaken by the review *L'Anneau d'Or*, and the many valuable publications on the meaning of Christian marriage.

[8] A. Brien, *Le cheminement de la foi* (Paris: Ed. du Seuil, 1964).

[9] We must cite here the works that treat of the renewal of the catechism, naming only the periodicals: *Catéchistes* (78 rue de Sevres, Paris VIIe), and *Parole et Mission* (Ed. du Cerf), and the 4th chapter of *Parole et Mission:* "L'Annonce de l'Evangile aujourd'hui" (Ed. du Cerf, 1962).

[10] P. Barrau, G. Matagrin, *Agir en vérité* (Paris: Ed. Ouvrieres, 1960).

spiritual studies on the mystery of Christ and the Church.[11] It has not feared to run a risk, and we dare not affirm that in all points it was able to avoid the drawback of presenting a theological consideration rather than a description of Christian existence. *Christus,* on the other hand, whose title is a program in itself, has chosen the various categories of Christian life, treating them in that promising perspective of reemphasizing the major values of the faith. The staff of *Christus* has not confined its efforts solely to maintaining the high quality of its own articles. It endeavors, by another collection of articles on similar subjects, to furnish the Christian with spiritual norms that are solidly and profoundly evangelical.

The book by J. Guillet, *Jésus-Christ, hièr et aujourd'hui,*[12] is indicative of this same point of view. Guillet presents Christ in his concrete mysteries in such a way that he becomes, through scrupulous fidelity to biblical intention, a pole of spiritual attraction. The Christological dogma which is the texture and meaning of Christian behavior draws thence its power of attraction and allurement; it becomes a spiritual force. Not only does the book affirm that there is no other way but Jesus Christ; it shows this in a palpable manner. The old categories of Christian existence rise up in the newness of their "Christic" origin. Certainly we do not claim that such works *completely* answer the problem which Christian existence poses—the withdrawal of large sections of the population from the sphere of religious and denominational influences. Certainly, however, this approach, a spirituality radically linked to the source of all faith (namely,

[11] *La Vie Spirituelle* (Ed. du Cerf, 1963-64), centered on the mysteries of Christ; 1964 centered on the mystery of the Church. The stand taken to recenter Christian behavior on objective faith appears to be too systematic and scholarly. It results moreover rather from a mental than a lived experience.

[12] J. Guillet, *Jesus Christ, Today and Yesterday* (London: G. Chapman, 1965). The review *Christus* to which this collection is added is published by the Society of Jesus (15 Rue Monsieur, Paris VIIe). *Laïcs et Vie chrétienne parfaite,* by C. Colombo, J. Giblet, B. Häring, L. Hausherr, S. Lyonnet, K. Truhlar (coll. *Laïcat et Sainteté;* University of Louvain). (Rome: Herder, 1963).

what we find in biblical revelation), is a partial answer to the problems of present-day Christian living.

The endeavor to reintegrate the "spiritual" with dogma, to turn it into the concrete form affirmed by revelation, appears to be the leading theme of the articles collected in Karl Rahner's book translated in the same *Christus* collection.[13]

These works, however, are limited, and this must not be held against them; their authors seem conscious of the fact. Their limitation is easily seen in that the reintegration of the spiritual into the heart of the mystery of faith risks turning the attention away from present difficulties in Christian living. Faith acknowledges this distress and surmounts it, for one of the concrete forms of faith is hope. Yet this distress is now experienced by human beings and the spiritual guidance we offer cannot disregard so widespread a situation.

Some may remember the last book of Reinhold Schneider, *Winter in Wien (Winter in Vienna)*.[14] It bears witness to the

[13] K. Rahner, *Elements de théologie spirituelle* (coll. Christus) (Paris: Desclée de Brouwer, 1964).

[14] R. Schneider, *Winter in Wien* (Vienna, 1958). (Cf. I. Goerres, "Incroyance du croyant," in *Signes des temps* IV, (April 1959). An analogous thought is found in the work of O. Rabut, *La vérification religieuse; recherche d'une spiritualité pour le temps de l'incertitude* (Paris: Ed. du Cerf, 1964). This may be judged from the following citation taken from the conclusion: "The Catholic Church is necessary; but it must have some latitude. And why not face up to reality: this latitude exists with or without her. It would prove a great liberation if the Church openly and gratefully acknowledged the legitimacy of doubting (*suspensive*) adherence (under certain spiritual conditions). Is a new era about to begin?"

"It is essential that the proposition of salvation be made known to all men in ways that do not go contrary to conscience. Moreover, the means of salvation considered as normal and seemingly necessary until the present day are inaccessible to a large number. A part of humanity is saved by ecclesial and traditional methods; but another part, at least an equal number, is not. Here we have a condition that must be recognized and settled. The Church is not reserved for one category of temperaments; therefore other methods must be found. It will take a long time; the Church, and rightly so, will not, except with great prudence, admit any new thing. But human beings beg for a right to be heard, especially those who in all sincerity are not convinced by all the statements of the Church; they insist that they be left the only type of faith from which they may expect salvation; a strict adhesion to funda-

feeling of dereliction which many believers experience. A meditation on history, it offers in a free form a thoughtful review of Europe's past, based on his experience in the winter of 1957-1958.

This meditation on history is Christian because it leads the author to question Christ. His interrogation is polemic, not peaceful. The Church is a source of appeasement in the agonizing darkness which God's silence engenders in history. Nevertheless, the Church dares not attempt to assume entirely the drama of contemporary man. Schneider wanted her to accept the cohabitation within her of belief and unbelief. Such a desire may be severely judged: it expresses the disorder and confusion in the face of God's implacable silence and the ineffectiveness of his witnesses in the course of a drama such as was the last war. There is no question of subscribing to this desire; it is good to understand it. In a passage of great beauty, Schneider makes us explore the tragic levels of Christian existence today; he wants Christ, agonizing and dying, to be preached in the Church, finding it an intolerable scandal that Christ in glory should be spoken of there. Such a proclamation hurls defiance at us who have tried to measure suffering. Let us be silent, he says, about the glory of Christ. It is alien to us. The truly human countenance of Christ, a man among men, is the narrow road toward hope.

We find that cry again in Mauriac's forward to Elie Wiesel's *La Nuit* [15] (*Night*). The young Israelite feels his faith weakening from the moment he encounters the unimaginable inhumanity of the Nazi death camps. "Never shall I forget that night, the first night after our capture, which made of my life a long night and a sevenfold imprisonment. Never shall I forget that smoke. Never shall I forget the faces of those little children whose bodies I saw transformed into curling columns of smoke under a mute blue sky. Never shall I forget those flames which con-

---

mental articles of faith does not exclude certain doubts. Their faith is troubled, a faith full of desire, of adherence to all that is pure and good. . . ." (*Op. cit.*, pp. 106-7).

[15] E. Wiesel, *Night* (New York, 1960).

sumed my faith forever. Never shall I forget that nocturnal
silence that took from me for all eternity my desire to live.
Never shall I forget those moments that murdered my God and
my soul, and my dreams that took on the aspect of the desert. . . ." And Mauriac adds: "I, I who believe that God is
love, what could I answer my young questioner whose blue eyes
reflected the angelic sadness on the face of the hanged child?
What could I have said to him? Could I have spoken of the
Israelite, that brother who resembled him perhaps, that Crucified
One whose cross had overcome the world? Could I have assured
him that the stone which the builders rejected had for me become
a cornerstone, and that the conformity between the cross and
man's suffering remains in my thought the key to that insoluble
mystery in which his childhood faith was lost? . . . We do not
know the price of a single drop of blood, a single tear. All is
grace. If the Eternal is the Eternal, the last word for each of us
belongs to him. There, that is what I should have said to the
little Jewish child. Instead I could only weep and embrace
him." [16]

All this seems to some people very far removed from spirituality. And in introductions to the spiritual life[17] it is not usual to
give much attention to the social and historical conditions for
the encounter with God in Jesus Christ, despite the high quality
of a few writers such as L. Bouyer. It seems to us that one of
the most characteristic ideas in contemporary spirituality is the
aim of integrating as one goes along the historical background
and social milieu that conditions a person's thought, action and
conduct. The work of Hans Urs von Balthasar, *Dieu et l'homme
aujourd'hui*,[18] seems to fulfill the requirement of modern Christian sensibility: Christian life cannot be studied without con-

---

[16] *Op. cit.*, pp. 12, 14.

[17] L. Bouyer, *Introduction to Spirituality* (New York: Desclée, 1961);
F. Roustang, *Une initiation à la Vie spirituelle* (coll. *Christus*) (Paris:
Desclée de Brouwer, 1963); P. Evdokimov, *The Ages of the Spiritual Life*
(Glen Rock, N.J.: Paulist Press, 1966). This is in the Orthodox tradition.

[18] H. Urs von Balthasar, *Dieu et l'homme aujourd'hui* (Paris: Desclée
de Brouwer, 1957).

sidering the general climate of life which influences the positive and negative relations with God. The individual's spiritual progress cannot be unrelated to the collective progress of society.

The problem presented to the mission of the Church by the increase of atheism in the world is a problem presented to each one. A person cannot live his relation with Christ at present the way he would have lived it in the days when faith in God was taken for granted. The dramatic aspect of witnessing to God by the Church in the world today involves somewhat the spirituality of each Christian. The progressive removal of many areas of human life from the influence of any religious denomination demands that Christian life be described in a different manner.

These developments have been very clearly perceived by Karl Rahner in *Mission et Grace*.[19] His manner of envisaging the new presence of Christianity in the world as "presence of the diaspora" has already had many repercussions in France: it is a rigorous interpretation of what has been the experience of many believers. This interpretation has not only a theological and pastoral value; it marks out a new line of action. The layman is no longer situated in a world filled with thousands of Christian institutions. The latter, in spite of many efforts to preserve them in their former dominating position, are dying out: in France they are being challenged by the most dedicated groups of the laity, at least in their present form. At the same time these groups feel a need for strengthening their faith. Living as they do in a world where the ecclesial horizon disappears now and again, they are seized with vertigo and cannot always keep in focus what is distinctively Christian.

In their constant devotion to struggling against injustice in its temporal forms, working with men and women who do not share their faith in Jesus Christ, often criticized slanderously and violently by those who do share their faith, some Christians do not discern any longer what their faith has to offer. They cling to it in the dark of night. Or else they are waiting for the day

[19] K. Rahner, *Mission et Grace* Vol. 1. Trans. as *Christian Commitment* by G. Hastings (New York: Sheed & Ward, 1963).

when they will be more courageously supported by the official Church in their effort to witness in a world that apparently denies God. The dramatic dimension of Christian life is not only linked to the silence of God, to the experience of death, to suffering and personal sense of failure; it is also written into the life of the visible Church. The struggle that has been going on for years on the part of laymen and priests for a Church that is less linked to certain non-evangelical forms, the struggle to have a free and prophetic Church that can make itself heard when grave questions are presented to the conscience of a nation, this is an exhausting struggle for spiritual life and the faith. Each one who has become involved in this struggle can ask himself fearfully whether he is on the right track, whether it would not be better to hold to the more traditional and assured paths. At this point the struggle for the faith is inseparable from the struggle for a new presence of the Church in the world. And this struggle which expresses the impatience of one who sees, must contain itself in patience: one must not get so far ahead of the whole troop that witness to the Gospel loses its ecclesial roots. The life of laymen and priests who take seriously the problems confronting the Church today is a constant battle sadly waged against the forces that threaten to overwhelm their faith: the world and the slowness of the official Church.

Christianity in losing its sociological foundations robs the believer of his superficial security. The "nights of faith" of which the mystical writers speak are experienced today in the difficulties of the Church. The events of these last years still ring loudly in the consciences of the most enlightened believers. It is not simply a question of those events having to do with the crisis about priest-workers, or with the still unsolved crisis of Catholic Action. Indeed, all these crises are significant, for they attest to the presence of Christianity in the world. But there is something else, something which extends beyond the official control of the Church. The success of a play such as "Der Stellvertreter" (The Deputy) [20] bears witness to this. The figure of

[20] R. Hochhuth, *The Deputy* (New York: Grove Press, 1964).

Pius XII is obviously a caricature that diminishes the vigor of the play, for the problem is only symbolically linked to the silence of Pius XII, and it persists in spite of all the posthumous justification that has been advanced. It is indeed concerned with Pius XII and it has to do with the prophetic power of the Church and of Christians. The destruction of the Jewish race, the horrible reality which we would like to forget today, did not take place in the Asiatic world, never Christianized; nor in the Communist world opposed to the Church; it took place entirely in Western Europe, in a country where Catholics are numerous, and in a country having a concordat with the Vatican. This panorama of "Christian" ineffectiveness in the drama of the Jews, recalled with crudity and more or less falsely presented in Hochhuth's play, is nevertheless always present in the consciousness of every clear-sighted believer. Is an institution whose mission is to testify in perfect freedom to the loving sovereignty of God so powerless with regard to its own faithful that it cannot open their eyes and influence them by a cry of protest, so that the strength of their convictions of faith will polarize the indignation of men confronting the inhumanity of man's intentions and actions? These questions, obscurely formulated, still weigh heavily on all spiritual thinkers. Ever since the historical and social dimensions of the Church have entered into relationship with Christ, faith finds security only in tearing itself away from the superficial security offered by the denominational institutions. By such means the Christian is led to the sole security of faith: the Word of God in Christ Jesus.[21]

The old foundations of Christian security are declining. We seek to understand this continual slipping away and the anguish it causes. Should not Christian life be understood in another way? And we begin to read about a man who in the Nazi prisons experiences the withdrawal of all those securities: "The problem of knowing what Christianity is, and who Christ is for us today,"

[21] P. A. Liégé, "L'Athéisme, tentation du monde, réveil des chrétiens," in *L'Athéisme, tentation du monde, réveil des chrétiens?* (Paris: Ed. du Cerf, 1963), pp. 229-51.

writes Bonhoeffer,[22] "constantly preoccupies me. The time when
everything could be said to men in theological or pious terms
has passed, as has the time of spirituality and conscience, that
is to say, the time of religion in general. We are about to enter
a totally irreligious epoch. As they are, men quite simply cannot
any longer be religious; even those who declare themselves to
be honestly religious do not in any way practice their religion;
they probably understand the word quite differently. All our
revelation and our Christian theology, nineteen centuries old,
rests on the 'religious a priori' of men. 'Christianity' has always
been one form of religion (perhaps the true one). If someday
it be discovered that this 'a priori' does not exist, but that it
was a form of expression of man depending on passing history,
if these men become radically irreligious—and I believe that that
is already more or less the case (how is it, for example, that this
war, unlike all others, does not call forth any religious reaction?)
—what then does this situation signify for Christianity? . . .

"If we have to regard the Western form of Christianity as the
entrance to complete irreligion, what will result for us, and for
the Church? The questions to which we must answer are these:
What does a Church, a parish, a liturgy, preaching, a Christian
life signify in a world without religion? How speak of God without religion, that is to say without the given preliminary and
presuppositions of metaphysics, spirituality, etc.? How speak
(or perhaps one should no longer speak as has been done until
now?) of God "laically"? How can Christians be irreligious and
profane? How form a Church without thinking of ourselves as
called, privileged on the spiritual level, but rather as belonging
entirely to the world? Christ then, would no longer be the object
of religion, but something quite different, really the Lord of the
world. But what does that signify? What do prayer and worship
signify in irreligiosity?"

These questions are born from the historic experience of the

[22] D. Bonhoeffer, *Résistance et Soumission; lettres et notes de captivité*
(Geneva, 1963), pp. 120-2; American edition: *Prisoner for God.* (New
York: The Macmillan Company, 1959).

Church, and that is why, without having any causal relationship, they fuse together from all sides. One cannot refute an historic experience. One surmounts it by a more all-embracing experience. This is still to come, and the thoughts expressed by Bonhoeffer and Robinson, no matter with what theological limits one may oppose them, express the present tearing apart of Christian existence.[23]

Does not the description of Christian experience as a drama mark a significant moment? Do not Christians recognize themselves more or less in the conclusions of Teilhard de Chardin? One could cite on this subject positive writings on the historical perspectives of the Church, even if the need for its reform is clearly indicated in them.[24] These essays do not contradict the testimony given by the works cited above, and it would be rash to see in Teilhard only a cheerful optimist. The dramatic dimension in these essays is noticeable in other ways: they are trying to see meaning in the progress of history. They do not say that this meaning is automatic, for it is never finished.[25] To discover the grandeur of what is ahead, and to measure the possibility of failing to reach it, make the tearing apart of Christianity very serious. It is not a question of despising the earth, nor does it consist in childish overconfidence in a collective movement for which no one is responsible and which no one can prevent. It has to do with placing collective and personal responsibility face to face with that which is possible. To accept this opportunity in order to root it in the flesh and blood of our history, that is our vocation as men and Christians. But faith does not put an end

[23] J. Robinson, *Honest to God* (Philadelphia: Westminster Press, 1963).
[24] M. D. Chenu, *L'Evangile dans le temps* (Paris: Ed. du Cerf, 1965). O. Rabut, *Valeur spirituelle du profane. Les Energies du monde et l'exigence religieuse* (Paris: Ed. du Cerf, 1962); A. Dondeyne, *La Foi écoute le monde;* C. Duquoc, *L'Eglise et le Progrès* (coll. l'Eglise aux cent visages), (Paris: Ed. du Cerf, 1964); F. Houtard, *L'Eglise et le Monde* (coll. l'Eglise aux cent visages), (Paris: Ed. du Cerf, 1964).
[25] This is emphasized in a different way by G. Martelet, *Victoire sur la Mort; Essai d'Anthropologie chrétienne* (Paris: Ed. Le Centurion, 1962). Let us mention also two works from *Lumière et Vie*: "Vivre dans le Monde" (50) and "La Mort" (68).

to uncertainty about the future if man refuses the invitation to what is marked out for him. The perception of a collective call to adapt our history in the human and Christian sense, does not make for security but turns back to that rending-apart of which we spoke above.

So it is that certain probings into contemporary spiritual literature lead us to recognize a new mode of Christian existence: it accepts what seems to be the direction of collective history, but it accepts in all seriousness the heartrending caused by the silence of God, the institutional delays of the Church, and the world's sin as it weighs on their faith. We are entering upon a time where impatience for efficacious action is now inscribed on a horizon of quiet patience, of infinite understanding of ecclesiastical delays, and of human misery. We are entering upon a time where clarity of thought does not kill action, and where the certitudes of faith never play false with man's doubts and uncertainties. The following text from St. Augustine describes marvellously well the spiritual situation about to come into being:

"Let those be angry with you who do not know the sighs and tears which the knowledge of the true God, even the most insignificant, exacts. Let them be roused against you, who have never been turned aside from their path, as you and I have been. As for me, it is absolutely impossible for me to be angry with you. . . .

"But so that you may never be vexed with me. . . . I must ask you a favor. Let us, you and me, do away with all arrogance. Let neither of us, neither you nor me, pretend to have discovered truth. Let us look for it as something equally unknown to both of us. We can then seek it with love and sincerity when neither of us has the boldness or presumption to believe it already in his possession. And if I cannot ask so much of you, grant me at least the favor of listening to you, of discussing with you, as with beings that I, for my part, do not pretend to know." [26]

[26] St. Augustine, *Contra Epistolam Manichaei* (cited by O. Rabut in "La Vérification religieuse," *op. cit.,* p. 109).

PART III

DO-C DOCUMENTATION

CONCILIUM

DIRECTOR: Leo Alting von Geusau
Groningen, Netherlands

ASS'T DIRECTOR: M.-J. Le Guillou, O.P.
Boulogne-sur-Seine, France

C. Murray Rogers/*Kareli, India*

Hindu Ashram Heritage: The Gift of God

As the opening chords of a Beethoven symphony stir an allusive memory and response in the heart and mind of many in western Europe, so the word "ashram" evokes an echo from the depths of his own being for millions of Hindus. However frustrating an experience it may be to Western man trained in the Aristotelian school, he may only properly consider the Indian ashram as institution and social structure when he has first "heard" it as primordial tone and melody. It rings from a time before recorded history and is one of those links of participation in the living past by which a Hindu carries the ineffable, the incommunicable, into his spiritual experience of the present moment. Only the man, from East or West, who lives with mystery and whose awareness has taught him that much in life—maybe most—can never be measured, can catch the overtones of music hidden in the word "ashram" for the believing Hindu.

To be "heard" first, and then seen: a clearing in the forest on the banks of a river, a little settlement of huts: under the pipal tree a rishi or holy man either sitting in contemplation or discoursing with one or two disciples; outside one of the nearby huts his elderly wife preparing a frugal meal. At the center of such a hidden community an altar and, on the altar, the sacred fire, agni. To such ashrams in the past emperors and kings have

143

gone barefoot and still today the great and important make the same journey, there to have the "darshan" of a soul "whose single glance can change a whole life" and "whose close-to-supernatural presence", as Arnaud Desjardins has said, is "the living witness of another world from that in which we live our lives".[1] Poets and musicians have described such a pilgrimage in word and song and the stone walls of many a Hindu temple tell the same tale.

A thousand and more years before St. Benedict wrote his rule describing the purpose of the monastic life as being "to seek God" (si revera quaerit Deum), these Hindu settlements or ashrams dotted the sub-continent. They were places where men and women lived in the greatest simplicity, under obedience to their spiritual guide or guru, and dedicated themselves to yearning and longing for God. It was of these that Pope Paul VI spoke when, as a pilgrim to this land in 1964, he said: "Yours . . . is the home of a nation that has sought God with a relentless desire, in deep meditation and silence, and in hymns of fervent prayer." In the same vein a sannyasi of Christ asks his fellow Christian how he could "remain indifferent to this call always further beyond, always further within, which the Spirit presents to him through India?" [2]

The root of the word "ashram" gives us a clue to the spiritual and physical environment of this intense desire to know, to experience, Brahman. "A-crama" (Sanskrit) means literally a place of exertion or asceticism for, although these forest or mountain settlements were indeed places of peace and silence. This was inseparable from the austerities and great simplicity and discipline which goes with spiritual endeavor and silent contemplation. As the years passed from the age of the Vedas to the times of the Mahabharata, "tapas" (mental and spiritual heat) took the place of the altar fire, "agni". The emphasis, however, on the persistent determination at whatever cost to

[1] A. Desjardins, Ashrams, les Yogis et les Sages (La Palatine, 1962); R. Girault, "Ashrams de l'Inde hauts lieux ou mirages?" in Parole et Mission (April, 1964).
[2] H. Le Saux, "L'Inde et le Carmel," in Carmel 1 (1965).

win detachment by submission, humility and hardship remained, and does remain until today.[3]

These places of daring spiritual experiments and of single-eyed concentration on interiority have given to India and the world not only the Upanishad but also Yoga, Samkya and Buddhism, not to speak of the countless souls whose spiritual yearning has driven them insatiably, during the past three millennia, to plunge into the interior Mystery and to seek the ineffable Presence.

During the centuries the extreme simplicity of structure has enabled the ashram to remain largely unaltered. Here the emphasis has been toward the hermitage and the solitary recluse, and there toward the cenobitic or conventual life. In both the pearl of Hinduism has been guarded and deepened, the vocation first to realize the Absolute and then to transmit this experience-beyond-all-words whose depths are never plumbed.

So hidden and secret is this treasure of India that very many from the West, and indeed in India, never see a trace of its presence. Others, privileged to meet signs of this inner life, follow the trail and are caught up in a lifetime's pilgrimage. Few are capable of hearing the true message of India in its utter purity, and even where glimpses of the depth of Hinduism are caught, as the present writer well knows, this unveiling is not of our deserving, nor even of our seeking; it is given, a gift of God.

So surprising, so unmerited! It was 1946; a priest and his wife from England landed at Bombay to be missionaries of Christ to India. They were members of the Anglican Church who previously, before marriage, had been raised in families of

---

[3] (a) For a fuller historical and critical study see P. Chenchiah, V. Chakkarai and A. Suarisanam, *Asramas Past and Present* (Madras: Indian Christian Book Club, 1941).

(b) The word "ashram" later came to refer to the four stages of the life of a Brahman:

(1) brahmacharya—the life of a student.
(2) grihastha—the life of a householder.
(3) vanaprastha—the time of retreat in the forest (vana).
(4) samnyasa—the last stage of life, the Wanderer.

(c) Readers, especially of the West, should note that the word "ashram" is frequently misused to mean a conference of a month's duration, or even a weekend; this is a sad prostitution of the word, greatly regretted by believing Hindus.

the strictest Protestant communions, one related to the Ana-
baptist denomination and the other a child of "Plymouth"
Brethren. They arrived in India with all the paraphernalia of
the typical Western missionary—the great quantity of luggage,
and the trappings that go with having two small children! There
was the other luggage of the West, the young, over-simplifying
West, the so frequently cocksure, abrupt, superior West. They
had come, as thousands like them, to give themselves and to
give the Gospel to India, "to bring Christ to India", "to convert
Hindus to Christ". Frightening phrases—as if Christ was not
present here until we Christians came, until his Church was
planted, as if conversion is the work of a human agent rather
than of the Spirit of God.

There followed four years of life and work in the almost
watertight, separate "Christian world" of India, a world largely
apart from Hindu life and faith and culture. True, forays were
made into that alien world but always to return to the Christian
compound, to the known ways of social life and custom, to the
Western prayer book, to Western hymns, to Western pre-supposi-
tions of thought, perception, spirituality.[4] There had indeed
been a certain modification in the more blatant polemic attitude
of Christian to non-Christian, but basically (and even today?)
it was still the polemic outlook, the spirit of the Crusades, however discreetly veiled, that held sway.

Looking back it seems as if the decisions which broke this
common pattern were so little in the hands of this English family.
An invitation came to join the Center of Basic Education
created by Mahatma Gandhi at Sevagram, his home and ashram
during the last years of his life, and this brought us into a community where, out of three hundred who lived and worked and
ate and worshiped together, only six were Christians. Who
could have guessed the inestimable privilege of being vulnerable,
of being *weak* as Christians? Later, a Hindu joint family opened

---

[4] The effects of Western Christianity in Asia are exposed critically and
sensitively by T. Ohm, *Asia Looks at Western Christianity* (Herder and
Herder, 1959).

its doors for us to enter as adopted members and for one year we lived in a one-room, mud and wattle house offered by this family. These outward changes were more than matched by inward changes, by the opening of the eyes, by the introduction into new "worlds" of thought and spirit, of feeling and appreciation as radical and surprising as—for a middle-class English family to find itself sitting on the floor of a one-room mud house in an Indian village.

Is revelation too strong a word? The revelation that came to us was of poverty, of real, grinding, material poverty, and with it the gradual discovery of a deep and genuine religious experience within Hinduism.[5] We began to appreciate, in the personal experience of meeting, the reality and joy of devotion and the trustful surrender of the bhatki, to sense the spiritual life which for countless Hindus is concretely centered on an "idol" which until then had so facilely been understood as a lower type of spirituality merely fit for destruction. We glimpsed also from afar the Advaita experience of the "Aham Brahmasmi", perhaps the highest spiritual experience possible outside Christian Faith, and underwent a certain synthesizing of these experiences while on actual pilgrimage to one of the sources of the Ganges high in the Himalayas; all these were profound and in many ways disturbing experiences.

There were, on the one hand, Europeans who had lost their Christian Faith in such encounters, and the pressure was great, especially from friends within the Gandhian Movement, for us to abandon living Christian Faith for a faith claiming to be so much more universal in appeal and answer. There were also others who, through such traumatic experiences, had rediscovered more deeply than ever before the reality of the living Christ and of the life of prayer. Until this time we had been

[5] For a sympathetic understanding of Eastern spirituality see J.-A. Cuttat, *The Encounter of Religions, a Dialogue between the West and the East* (Desclée, 1960); J. Monchanin and H. Le Saux, *Ermites du Saccidânanda* (Casterman, 1956). This has particular reference to Advaita; P. Deleury, *Toukaram: Psaumes du Pèlerin,* is an excellent book on the faith and devotion of the bhakti.

able to "touch bottom" but now, out of our depth, we were to discover whether or not we could swim.

As if to underline the appeal and pressure of Hindu friends, there began to appear on our horizon Hindu holy men and women whose depth and holiness could only be denied—at least so it seemed to us—by calling black white. There was Ramana Maharshi of Tiruvanamalai whom we came to know through his writings and poems, and later through one who knew him personally, Swami Abhishiktesvarananda; there were others such as Ma Anandamayi of Varanasi and Swami Ramdas of Kanhangad, Kerala,[6] and we went on to discover that this "secret" was shared not only by the few famous sages of India but by countless unknown souls. They together share "this implacable experience of the Presence which for centuries and millennia has thrown so many sons of India into the most a-cosmic vocation one could imagine, as they wander from village to village . . . scarcely speaking except sometimes to remind those whom they meet of the secret self within . . . or else remaining hidden in the solitudes of forests or in mountain caves, the attention fixed within, simple witnesses of the One".[7]

Still more. There were the religious scriptures by which millions of Hindus still live, the Upanishad and the Bhagavad Gita, and the scriptures written in stone in the Ajanta or Elephanta Caves. Who can stand before the magnificent Shiv in the latter without an awareness of the depth of faith from which it sprang. Such depth was to find expression centuries later in the new Cathedral in Coventry, England, according to its architect, Sir Basil Spence. These all swelled the wave under which the Christian was drowned or upon which he was lifted to discover the

[6] B. Narasimhaswamy, *Self Realization, Life and Teachings of Sri Raman Maharshi;* Sri Ramana Gita, *Teachings of Bhagavan Sri Ramana Maharshi;* these works, together with poems and hymns, are obtainable from Sri Ramanas-raman, Tiruvanamalai, South India; *Words of Sri Anandamayi Ma* (1961); *God-experience* (Bombay: Bhavan Books, 1963) for the teachings of Swami Ramdas.

[7] "Swami Abhishiktesvarananda": Unpublished section of *L'Inde et le Carmel* (cf. *supra* n. 2).

towering heights of Christ's Lordship of which he was previously
but dimly aware.

Slowly, but very surely, this experience of living Hinduism
proved to be a catalyst to our Western Christian life and spirit.
How could we any longer deny that within this ancient and still
living Hindu "world" God himself, Father, Son and Spirit had
always been at work drawing this vast section of the human
family toward himself? It was indeed this awareness that there
are treasures of the Spirit of God within Hinduism, a most
precious pearl that perhaps will become one of the most glorious
in the crown of the Catholic Church of Christ, that resulted in
an invitation to pilgrimage, pilgrimage into the love of God
little dreamed of when we arrived in Bombay in 1946.

Thus it was that there began to be born in 1954 a Christian
Ashram called Jyotiniketan, Place of Uncreated Light. We were
no longer to be one natural human family but to await God's
gift of a family of those men and women whom he would give
us in Christ. The call to meet, worship and love Christ from
within the human situation of poverty and from within the so
largely hidden and deep spiritual "world" of Hinduism led us
clearly to our chief work—the worship and love of God, the
Blessed Trinity. This alone was to be our work, not the preliminary to some other work, no matter how necessary and
right for other Christian hands. Owing to our spiritual inade-
quacy, then as now, we could not see precisely where this community life for the worship of God would lead, but we could
see the stretch of road just ahead and that was and is more than
enough for today. The rest is known to God.

So our calling, however often it may overwhelm us, is to bear
witness to the supernatural presence, that God himself may be
known ever more deeply by ourselves and by our neighbors,
to be, here between these two villages of north India, himself,
adorable, incomprehensible, all-embracing. Men assuredly need
medicine, education, better agriculture, but that must be the
task of others. Our calling is to place before men the super-

natural, to open a window on divine reality, to let the marvel of the Transfiguration of our Lord become again a living and contemporary reality in this small corner of his universe.

Our Protestant upbringing had not led us to look with any particular favor upon monasticism, but now, to our great surprise, we found ourselves led to it through Hinduism! Our *raison d'être* (to love God in community) has brought us to see more clearly as the years have passed that such a way of love requires the receiving of God's gifts of simplicity, obedience and a life for unity. No outward vows are made; a serious inward and outward commitment is asked of each member, after a lengthy period of testing and preparation, for "marriage" to this life in community. This commitment is made to God and to one another for an unlimited period, that is, until death. We share our goods and our money, none of which comes from abroad for it is clear to us that if we would live deeply within this world where God has placed us it must be from *this* world, *this* earth, and with *this* people that God intends us to live.

The life of each day, beginning with silent worship at 5:20 a.m., and ending with the Christarakhjshja and the Kiss of Peace at the end of Compline at 8:30 p.m., centers in the worship of God in the House of Prayer. The holy eucharist, in which the Lord so wonderfully gives us himself, and by which we are allowed to share in the creating, redeeming, divinizing of this corner of the world, is the Living Center of our life and the deepest act we may perform for our neighbors, though we are only now beginning to live in this reality. This life in Christ is continued outside the chapel in work in the fields and houses, study in the ashram library, simple service to village friends, regular periods of silence in three small huts set aside for this purpose, and our times of conversation with frequent guests and visitors.

From the beginning we have known that Jyotiniketan is for Christians of any communion—our full members now include three Anglicans and one Presbyterian—and one of the greatest of God's gifts to us has been friends of widely differing allegiance: Roman Catholics, members of the ancient Oriental Churches, of Churches of the Reformation and of fundamentalist groups. We have asked from others as from ourselves the fullest loyalty to that communion to which each belongs and a genuine respect for the convictions and conscience of the other, no matter how hard and painful this may be.

In the founding of Jyotiniketan ashram our inspiration had come through the Gandhian Movement and from Hindu sources through which we believed the Spirit to be speaking to us. The ecclesiastical authorities of this Anglican diocese had given us their prayers and their blessing. Only later did it become fully apparent to us just how un-original we had been!

Roberto de Nobili, toward the end of 1607 from a dilapidated hut near the Temple of Siva in Madurai, which served as his ashram as he began his life as a sannyasi, wrote in a personal letter: "I am now living in a cabin with earthen walls and a thatched roof, which is more useful to me and makes me happier than if it were a rich palace. . . . I always remain confined to my little cabin. After rising and saying Mass and commending myself to the Lord, I admit anyone who wishes to come to talk or discuss with me." [8] His innate courtesy and deep wisdom drew many Hindus while, most painfully, his fellow Christians filled his life with difficulties. We in the 20th century who have experienced something of the same call but under circumstances so much easier, look back with marvelling respect to de Nobili; he laid the foundation of our work.

Grass grew over then! More than three centuries passed before Christian ashrams began to appear in South India. In 1921 Christukula Ashram, interdenominational in character, was founded in Tirupattur by two medical doctors, one an Indian and the other a Scot. In 1928 the Christa Prema Seva Sangna, an Anglican ashram with its patron St. Francis of Assisi, began in Poona;[9] in 1937 the Christa Sishya Sangna at Tadagam

---

[8] Vincent Cronin, *A Pearl to India: The Life of Roberto de Nobili* (London: Rupert Hart-Davis, 1959).

[9] This ashram has now, regrettably, ceased to exist.

was the first Christian ashram community in which the family was to find its due place. This last was open to priests and lay people, married and unmarried, most of whom belonged to the Orthodox Syrian Church of Malankara. It had as one of its foundation members the Anglican Bishop Pakenham Walsh. In addition to these there have been some fifteen to twenty similar ashrams, all except two situated in South India, related to the Mar Thoma Church of Malabar, to the Church of South India or to the Anglican Church.

No one would deny the devoted service which has been offered, largely to village people, by the members of these ashrams but it has to be admitted that the high hopes attendant on their formation have not been as yet fulfilled. It was intended that these centers might "acclimatize the Gospel in India",[10] that Christian evangelism expressed through ashrams would be more palatable to Hindus, that the Gospel could in this way be more effectively proclaimed and that Christian social work could be made more readily acceptable. Unfortunately it was not sufficiently realized that such intentions themselves spring from a Western understanding of Christianity which almost inevitably sees the ashram as a means to an end, as a method of work and evangelism, and consequently puts the greater weight on the external work of preaching and social service rather than on the contemplative vocation of the traditional Indian ashram. The inability to accept sacramental obedience as a gift of God, and the plan by which members commit themselves for a limited number of years, and not normally for life, have resulted in an instability in these ashrams which has not yet been overcome.

It was not until 1950 that a Christian ashram was founded in the profound Hindu tradition—for a group of men to lead "the contemplative life in the pristine tradition of Christian monasticism and the closest possible conformity to the traditions of the Indian sannyasa".[11] This was the Roman Catholic ashram of

[10] S. Neill, *Christian Missions* (Penguin Books, 1964). Short section on the Ashram Movement.

[11] For Saccidânanda Ashram see: *Swami Parama Arubi Anandam: (Fr. J. Monchanin) a Memorial* (Saccidânanda Ashram, 1959) and

Saccidânanda on the banks of the Kavery River in South India, founded by Swami Parama Arubi Anandam (Father Jules Monchanin) and Swami Abhishiktesvarananda (Dom M. le Saux). Here in silence and hiddenness the "re-capitulation" (the Anakephalaiōsasthai of Ephesians 1, 10), the "gathering together in one all things in Christ" would be the work of sannyasis or contemplative monks. Their vocation would be to gather up for Christ India's deepest spiritual heritage and to allow the death and resurrection with Christ (part of this great gift of our Hindu brethren) to happen within the heart of the Christian contemplative, the representative of Christ's eschatological Church in India. "It would be mere Pharisaism for the believer were he to be content with preaching to his Hindu brother the necessity of dying in order to rise again with Christ. It is for the Christian first of all to realize in himself this mystic death in the very name of his brother." [12] The death of Father Monchanin in 1957 has by no means extinguished this vision; his companion, waiting patiently for the spark to catch among Indian Catholics, continues the pilgrimage.

Here in Jyotiniketan, as a gift of God, certain currents seem to be flowing together whose future course or strength cannot be assessed. Our shared meeting with Hindu spirituality has given us an ecumenical experience with Roman Catholic Christians of a depth far beyond our expectations and has led us to reevaluate our Anglican-Protestant traditions. Three of our annual retreats have been led by Roman Catholic friends and a circle formed, composed of Orthodox, Roman Catholic, Anglican and Protestant members; it has met on four occasions under the leadership of Dr. Jacques-Albert Cuttat. [13] Of one of these

---

Ermites du Saccidânanda (cf. *supra* n. 5). Mention may also be made of a more recent experiment at Kurisumala, Kerala, where an Eastern monastery following the pattern of the Cistercian life was founded in 1958. See article by Dom B. Griffiths, in *Eastern Churches Quarterly* 3 (1964).

[12] Swami Abhishiktetsvarananda, "Rencontre avec l'Hindouisme," in *Inf. Cath. Intern.* (August, 1964).

[13] Reports on "circle" meetings on Hindu and Christian spirituality: On meetings 2 and 3, J. Britto (Dharmaram College, Bangalore); on meeting

meetings a member has written: "By the call of the Spirit through India to the deepest interior center of a man's being they discovered each other to be Christians on a level of truth and at a depth where all apparent divisions were transcended. 'The anamnesis of the Church before the time of separations', murmured one of them in astonishment." [14] It is too early yet to speak in any definitive way of where this may lead in spiritual or theological terms but it is clear that the Spirit calls us to step out into new paths which will require a blending of courage and a deep loyalty to the Faith of the Church.

Four matters insistently demand further thought, prayer and obedient response. Firstly, the insatiable thirst of Hinduism for the One, the Absolute, beyond words, beyond images, reminds us forcibly of the absolute supremacy of contemplation. If this, the precious pearl of Hinduism, is to be assumed, to find its fullness in Christ, then we Christians of India (of the world?) must needs rediscover this depth. The swami of Saccidânanda Ashram has truly said: "The secret of India will only pass over to the Church by a transmission, ontological as it were, from depth to depth, from soul to soul in the great silence." [15] India from her depth calls the Church to her depth and "above all it is not contemplatives in name or title that the Church and India need but souls plunged into the mystery of the within, no matter what name or title they bear". Have we not too often dissipated our Christian energies, our love, on the many while "the one thing needful" (Luke 10, 42) has been sadly neglected?

Secondly, by the unveiling to us of the Spirit's footprints within Hinduism a double realization begins to dawn. Christ Pantocrator, the cosmic Christ, requires us to meet him not only at the "end" of Hinduism but at its beginning, to discover the fulfillment of the cosmic covenant with Noah and the signifi-

---

3, cf. footnote 12; on meeting 4, see the article in *Kairos* (1965), and the article by M. Kalapesi in *Religion and Society* (a publication of the Christian Institute for the Study of Religion and Society, 19 Miller Road, Bangalore, India).

[14] Cf. footnote 12.

[15] Cf. footnote 2.

cance of Melchizedek, the priest-king, in and through the millennia of strivings on the part of rishi and sannyasi of this country. The concomitant of this, as Dr. Raymond Panikkar has said, is to accept with all its implications for the mission of the Church that "the Christian attitude is not ultimately one of bringing Christ *in,* but of bringing him *forth,* of discovering Christ; not one of command but of service". The Christian has in this way to cooperate in God's redemption, in the "lifting of the veil, a thick veil of centuries, covering the dust of history and the stains of sin".[16] This task will not be performed without much pain, sacrifice and even conflict.

Furthermore, the new relationship between Christianity and Hinduism which is being pressed upon us demands of us a radical rooting out of the polemical approach which for long has supported the missionary work of the Church. This asks of us nothing less than a thorough conversion in ourselves; our self-importance needs to be rooted out and we need once more, and again and again, to become slaves of the Gospel. We do not propose the ending of polemics because we live in an age of tolerance (when this method is no longer successful), but precisely because Christ himself, the redeemer of the whole world including this Hindu "world" comes "to gather into one the children of God who are scattered abroad" (John 11, 52), not to wage war on them. Are we not therefore called in all seriousness to renounce every tendency in ourselves to gain a victory over another faith? Rather our calling is to bear the heavy responsibility of being prophets and priests of Hinduism, and, with deep sensitiveness and love—always deeply rooted in Christ—to open ourselves to the living spiritual experience of Hinduism. Thus, going deeper than theologies, dogmas and doctrines, we shall experience the metanoia of, and with, the Hindu into Christ himself, the Alpha and Omega of every religion and culture as of every individual person.

[16] R. Panikkar, *The Unknown Christ of Hinduism* (London: Darton, Longman and Todd, 1964). An invaluable study which contains a full bibliography.

Finally, if this task is to be fulfilled, then we are led to move toward a wider ecumenism, an ecumenism which is indeed catholic, universal, concerned not only in the dialogue and encounter between Christians of different confessions but also between members of different religions. Christian unity awaits not only the miracle of God's uniting gift in the life of the Blessed Trinity to Roman Catholics, Orthodox, Anglicans and Protestants, but also to "other believers" including that great section of mankind who describe themselves as Hindus. Only the universe, the universal in Christ, can satisfy man's God-given yearning for unity.[17]

The Christian ashram is no place for easy and compact answers. It is a place where Christian men are being confronted by the Absolute, across barriers of denominational loyalty, indeed across centuries of inter-religious antagonism and rivalry; they are faced with questions which may well change radically our understanding of life in Christ, and which may, if answered with an always deeper abandonment to the living Lord, allow us a real part in the Passover of Hinduism into its promised land, into Christ. Such is our fearful and exhilarating responsibility. Brethren, please, pray for us.

[17] C. Murray Rogers, "Monde Hindou et unité en Christ," in *Semences d'Unité* (Casterman, 1965).

PART IV

CHRONICLE OF THE
LIVING CHURCH

In Collaboration with
Katholiek Archief
Amersfoort, Netherlands

The Latin-American Church and the Development of Socio-Religious Research

The Church in Latin-American countries significantly has favored socio-religious research more than in other countries. In fact organizational centers now exist in five countries: Mexico, Colombia, Chile, Argentina and Brazil. However, equally important work has been realized elsewhere. Latin America is the first continent where a regional secretariat of the International Federation of Institutes for Socio-Religious Research (FERES) has been established, with an office in Bogotá, which distributes an Information Bulletin.[1] It is also the only continent where a series of coordinated studies has been completed.[2]

How do we account for this situation? What elements have been at work in favor of such a position, and for what reasons does the Church utilize this instrument of understanding?

Origins

In asking such questions, it should be understood that to speak of a Latin-American Church is somewhat arbitrary. More im-

[1] *Boletin d'information*—FERES—Latin America, Apdo aereo 11.966, Bogotá, Colombia.
[2] Studies published in forty volumes by FERES and condensed in F. Houtart and E. Pin, *L'Eglise a l'heure de l'Amerique latine* (Casterman, Paris, Tournai, 1965); or F. Houtart and E. Pin, *The Church in the Latin-American Revolution* (New York: Sheed & Ward, 1965).

159

portant than any geographical distinction is the fact that it exists in the midst of a "typology" of social and pastoral attitudes. Thus it is necessary to explore the origins of the interest in, the indifference toward, and the rejection of a course that implies socioreligious research.

The chief source of interest stems from the rapid social change which the Latin-American continent is undergoing. This condition has provoked confusion about traditional social structures, and questioning in regard to a great number of values upon which this society has been constructed.

A certain number of bishops, priests and laymen have perceived this problem very rapidly. Not only have they seen, through fidelity to the Gospel, the necessity of taking new social positions and initiatives, but they have also realized that this changing course of action will radically alter the position of the Church, the direction of her mission, her pastoral method and the definition of various roles (priest, laymen, and religious men and women).

Among these people, interest in a deeper study of the situation on the continent is rapidly being manifested. However, the early confusion regarding a course of action has produced disorder. Not only is it not known how to attack these problems, but there has often existed an incapacity for analyzing the problem. For this reason, during the discussion on Schema 13, Most Rev. Benitez, Auxiliary Bishop of Asunción in Paraguay, speaking on behalf of 115 Latin-American bishops, proposed that the studies of FERES presented a rapid analysis of the social situation on the continent, and would serve as a basis for discussion on doctrinal positions. This confidence in analysis has impressed several African and Asian bishops.

Among those who have been awakened to the profound changes in Latin-American society, some have concerned themselves chiefly with the social and cultural aspects. They have expressed a desire for studies to clear the way for relatively prompt action. They have often shown little interest in the studies of religious sociology as such, partly because social action seems more urgent to them, but more particularly because they have not perceived profound instances of social change in the Church as an institution.

Such indifference toward socio-religious studies often is accompanied by a certain immobility, either in an intellectual vacuum or with a pastoral dedication quite diligent but isolated, overburdened, and performed in bits and pieces outside the normal channels of communication.

Opposition to this type of work, notably in the domain of religious sociology, often arises from a particular position on the definition and functions of the Church, usually accompanied by a characteristic absence of information about the real situation. This attitude is typical of people who believe that the Church dominates the society, possesses all the truth, and is consequently always right—there is nothing else that she can possibly learn.

It is necessary to add that, thanks to these reciprocal influences, certain studies have aided the discovery of social and pastoral problems on the continent. As a result this movement goes on uninterrupted.

Finally, the existence of CELAM, the Latin-American Episcopal Conference, has played an important role in the development of socio-religious studies. The delegates from national episcopal conferences were sent by many bishops particularly conscious of the problems of social change. These delegates were, in general, more clearly enlightened than the episcopal sees which they represent. The greater portion of the annual meetings were devoted to studies more or less based on socio-religious documents and accounts on the family, vocations, pastoral activity, etc., according to the topics under discussion each day.

This same organization has also conducted such studies along the lines of a continental project. This method not only aids the exchange of ideas but also the elaboration of study programs at the same level.

Expectations

The expectations of the Church in Latin America are clearly seen in her desire for service through action rather than theoretical reflection. This attitude is easily understandable, for everyone—laymen, priests and bishops—is confronted with numerous and urgent problems. We might point out four chief areas of attention.

The first is the need for *more precise information.* It is this need, for example, that led the two vice-presidents of CELAM to ask FERES, before the last session of the Council, to publish a brochure reviewing the research carried out on the continent and to distribute it to the Latin-American bishops.[3] Subsequently, this brochure was also published in French and English in order to inform the bishops of other continents at the second session of the Council.

It is this same preoccupation which induced Cardinal Silva Henriquez of Santiago (Chile) to encourage a survey of public opinion about the Church and which induced CELAM to request actual research on the liturgical renewal in Latin America.

Studies are also under way on the orientation of *social and pastoral action.* Brazil presents an interesting example for this point of view. CERIS, the Center for Statistics and Socio-Religious Research,[4] works in conjunction with the National Episcopal Conference and regional conferences, for the elaboration of pastoral projects and for the organization of comprehensive pastoral work. Similarly IMES, the Mexican Institute of Social Studies, works in collaboration with 20 dioceses united in their desire for common pastoral thinking and action. A final example is the archdiocese of Bogotá which initiated a study on the city for the purpose of strengthening comprehensive pastoral work.

Such projects are also utilized to serve as a *basis of formation* for both clergy and active laymen. In pastoral discussions, in the

[3] F. Houtart, *La Iglesia latino-americana en la hora del Concilio* (FERES, 1962).
[4] This organization also publishes an information bulletin: *Boletin Informativo,* Rio de Janeiro.

courses of the Higher Institute of Pastoral Activity (ISPLA) and in a number of seminaries and formation courses, socio-religious projects form a basis for greater understanding and pastoral reflection.

Finally (and some bishops are very sensitive in this case), these projects serve as a basis for *theological reflection,* together with Christian social and pastoral action. The particular problems arising from unreasonable demands for development, from the lack of priests and from the new roles given to the laity, to future dioceses and to religious, etc., all demand theological thought as a reference for concrete situations in Latin America. At the instigation of CELAM an initial effort has taken shape in the form of a common project among theologians and sociologists designed chiefly for Latin-American bishops, and published during the second session of the Council.[5]

Orientations

In the majority of cases, it is known that socio-religious research is utilized not only to reconsider purely ecclesial structures, but ultimately to orientate the social responsibility of both Christians in general and the institutional Church in particular. The fact that research centers occasionally have different sections (socio-economic and socio-religious) and the existence of an organization such as DESAL (Center for Social Development in Latin America), with its office in Chile, demonstrate that perspectives go beyond pure religion.

Evidently, the utilization of results and the orientation of research depend upon the perspectives of those who actually employ them. Thus, their findings at times might be judged as transcending the point of view of actual theological thought on the role of the hierarchy in social life.

The centers now in operation are also preoccupied with more fundamental research. That is why they have made contacts with religious sociologists, both in Europe and in North America, in order to explore more deeply the theoretical aspects of studies in

[5] FERES, *Las Tareas de la Iglesia en America latina* (Bogotá, 1963).

the Church in the midst of social change. This preoccupation envisages the religious fact not only as an element submitting to change but also as a factor of change, or, in sociological terminology, as an independent variable. It is with this in mind that FERES has inaugurated two very important studies, one on northeastern Brazil and the other on the Church as an institution in the midst of social change in Latin America.

We can conclude that the attitude of the Latin-American Church on socio-religious research is consonant with its attitude in all other areas. However, because of a certain dynamic stream, there has been particular interest in this discipline, and this is of particular importance in the midst of a rapidly changing situation.

BIOGRAPHICAL NOTES

CHRISTIAN PAUL ANDRÉ DUQUOC, O.P.: Born December 22, 1926 in Nantes, joined the Dominicans and was ordained in 1953. He studied at the University of Fribourg, at the Saulchoir (Paris) and at the Ecole Biblique, Jerusalem. Since 1957 he has taught dogmatic theology as a member of the theological faculty in Lyons, and he is Visiting Professor at the Institute of Religious Studies of the University of Montreal. He is the author of *L'Eglise et le Progrès* (Ed. du Cerf) and contributes frequently to *Lumière et Vie,* of whose editorial board he is a member.

ALBERT-MARIE BESNARD, O.P.: Born March 27, 1926 in Toulouse, joined the Dominicans, and was ordained in 1954. He studied philosophy and theology at the Saulchoir (Paris). From 1957-59 he was Prior of the Dominican House in Strasbourg, from 1959-1964 Novice Master of the Order's House in Lille, and since 1964 has been Master of Studies in the Saulchoir novitiate. His publications include *Le pélérinage chrétien* (Ed. du Cerf, 1959), *Le mystère du Nom* (Ed. du Cerf, 1962), *Visage spirituel des temps nouveaux* (Ed. du Cerf, 1964), and he contributes articles to *La Vie Spirituelle, Lumière et Vie,* etc.

FRANÇOIS VANDENBROUCKE, O.S.B.: Born May 20, 1912 in Brussels, joined the Benedictines and was ordained in 1938. Having studied at Louvain, he holds various professorships, is a Novice Master, and an Editor of the journal *Questions Liturgiques et Paroissiales,* to which he is a regular contributor. Publications include *Le Mission dans l'Eglise du Christ* (Louvain, 1947), *Les Psaumes et le Christ* (Louvain, 1955), *Direction spirituelle et hommes d'aujourd'hui* (Paris, 1955), and *La Spiritualité du moyen âge* (Paris, 1961); he wrote the latter in collaboration with J. Leclercq, O.S.B., and Louis Bouyer, Cong. Orat. A translation is in preparation with Burns & Oates and will form the second volume in their projected four-volume *History of Spirituality.*

PAUL MIKAT: Born December 10, 1924 in Germany. He studied at Bonn University where he became Doctor of Law in 1954. He has held, and still holds, numerous academic posts in Germany as well as various offices in German central and local government.

EDOUARD ADRIEN RANWEZ: Ordained in 1906. He became Professor of Philosophy and Spiritual Director at the seminary at Floreffe and from 1921-1955 was Professor of Moral, Ascetic and Mystical Theology at the Namur seminary. He is the author of *Morale et Perfection* (1959) and numerous articles.

AGNES CUNNINGHAM, S.S.C.M.: Born in Middlesborough (England) on May 26, 1923 and joined the Servants of the Holy Heart of Mary. She studied at the Gregorian Institute of America, the University of St. Louis, Marquette University, and at Lyons, gaining a bachelor's degree in Church music and English literature, a master's degree in theology, and a licentiate in theology. She is at present engaged in the educational apostolate of her Congregation and is an Instructor in Theology at Mundelein College, Chicago.

ETIENNE MICHEL CORNÉLIS, O.P.: Born in Belgium on April 11, 1915, joined the Dominicans, and was ordained in 1950. He studied at the Universities of Brussels and Liège and at the Saulchoir, where he gained his doctorate in theology in 1958, having previously qualified in mathematics, history and Oriental literature. He holds various professorships, including that of Professor of the History of Religions and Philosophy of Religion in the Theological Faculty at Nijmegen. His publications include *La Libération de l'homme dans les Religions non-chrétiennes* (1958), *Les fondements cosmologiques de l'eschatologie d'Origène* (1959), and *La gnose éternelle* (1959—with A. Léonard). He is a contributor to *Tijdschrift voor Theologie, Supplément de la Vie Spirituelle, Recherches des Sciences Philosophiques et Théologiques,* etc.

G. NEYRAND: Born in Lyons in 1920 and ordained in 1950. He translated into Japanese the *Letters of St. Ignatius of Antioch.*

HANS URS VON BALTHASAR: Born in 1905 in Lucerne, Switzerland. He studied Germanic languages and philosophy in Zurich, earning a doctorate for his study of "The Eschatalogical Problem in German Literature". Many of his works have been translated into English, including: *St. Therèse of Lisieux* (Sheed & Ward, 1953), *Elizabeth of Dijon* (Pantheon, 1956), *Prayer* (Sheed & Ward, 1961), *Theology of History* (Sheed & Ward), and *Martin Buber and Christianity* (Macmillan).

C. MURRAY ROGERS: Born in 1917. He took his B.A. and M.A. at the University of Cambridge, followed by a theological degree (also at Cambridge) and a diploma in education at London University. Ordained in the Anglican ministry in 1941, he held a post with the Church Missionary Society till 1946, when he took up the first of several important missionary posts in India, where at present he works with the Jyotiniketan Ashram.

International Publishers of CONCILIUM

ENGLISH EDITION
Paulist Press
Glen Rock, N. J., U.S.A.

Burns & Oates Ltd.
25 Ashley Place
London, S.W.1

DUTCH EDITION
Uitgeverij Paul Brand, N. V.
Hilversum, Netherlands

FRENCH EDITION
Maison Mame
Tours/Paris, France

GERMAN EDITION
Verlagsanstalt Benziger & Co., A.G.
Einsiedeln, Switzerland

Matthias Grunewald-Verlag
Mainz, W. Germany

SPANISH EDITION
Ediciones Guadarrama
Madrid, Spain

PORTUGUESE EDITION
Livraria Morais Editora, Ltda.
Lisbon, Portugal

ITALIAN EDITION
Editrice Queriniana
Brescia, Italy